Kids

who think
outside
the box

Helping Your Unique Child Thrive
in a Cookie-Cutter World

Stephanie Lerner

AMACOM
AMERICAN MANAGEMENT ASSOCIATION
New York | Atlanta | Brussels | Chicago
Mexico City | San Francisco | Shanghai
Tokyo | Toronto | Washington, D. C.

Special discounts on bulk quantities of AMACOM books are available to corporations, professional associations, and other organizations. For details, contact Special Sales Department, AMACOM, a division of American Management Association, 1601 Broadway, New York, NY 10019.
Tel.: 212-903-8316. Fax: 212-903-8083.
Web site: www. amacombooks.org

This publication is designed to provide accurate and authoritative information in regard to the subject matter covered. It is sold with the understanding that the publisher is not engaged in rendering legal, accounting, or other professional service. If legal advice or other expert assistance is required, the services of a competent professional person should be sought.

Quotations from Gail McGougan and Deborah Hardy are used with permission.

Library of Congress Cataloging-in-Publication Data

Lerner, Stephanie Freund.
Kids who think outside the box : helping your unique child thrive in a cookie-cutter world / Stephanie Freund Lerner.
   p.   cm.
   Includes bibliographical references and index.
   ISBN 0-8144-7275-3
1. Exceptional children.   2. Individuality in children.   3. Successful people—Biography.   4. Exceptional children—Services for—United States—Directories.   I. Title.
HQ773.5.L47   2005
649'.15—dc22   2004024925

Printing number

10 9 8 7 6 5 4 3 2 1

Kids

who think
outside
the box

I dedicate this book to all those kids who are
unique in thought, spirit, and personality.

The key to your success and personal greatness
is the wisdom and conviction
of knowing who you are . . . and holding the course.

To my three children—
Morgen, Chelsae, and Spencer . . .
You hold the course every day!
I learn from you.

CONTENTS

Part Three
THE SOURCE BOOK: Exceptional Programs,
Adventures, and Voyages for Your Child:

FOREWORD

THE IMPORTANCE OF INDIVIDUALITY

AND THINKING DIFFERENTLY

WHETHER I WAS teaching preschool, kindergarten, first grade or graduate school, almost every year, for more than 20 years, there would be one student who moved to his or her own beat. Whereas most students followed the crowd and succumbed to peer pressure, these few individuals were content, or perhaps determined, to do their own thing. They thought individually, uniquely, and what could be considered *outside the box*.

That *thing* that they were determined to do—whether it was Drew's interest and knowledge of trains, Paige's interest in tennis, Carolyn's interest in math and numbers, Jeremy's interest and knowledge of animals, or Nathaniel's fascination with dinosaurs—was to follow a *passion*. It was a focus that guided them throughout their school year. This focus did not make these students aloof and unpopular with their peers; in fact, their peers often looked up to them as experts in their "fields"—even in preschool and kindergarten. Their interests were occasionally passing fancies that lasted all or part of one school year, but sometimes these interests became self-motivated, lifelong studies.

Over the years I have come to realize that the major characteristic these individuals shared was not related to IQ, socioeconomic status, ethnicity, or personality type, but to parental and teacher encouragement. When a parent, or teacher, acknowledges and encourages a child's interest, it fosters feelings of self-esteem and self-worth. It reinforces that significant adults respect and value their interests, which serves as the foundation for furthering the student's desire to learn, discover, and explore. Such encouragement provides the unique and individual child with the confidence to go forth and be the person that he or she is with fortitude and self-assurance.

The importance of parental support as the crucial underpinning of a child's eventual success is demonstrated by the many stories contributed by *eminent achievers* to this book. Neil deGrasse Tyson, head of the Hayden Planetarium in New York City and one of these eminent achievers, followed his pursuit of astronomy and the stars with the support of his parents. Spike Lee recognizes his mother's expectations and standards as a significant element in his success. Many other notable participants refer to beneficial parental support in their narratives, which leaves the reader with the feeling that positive parental support played a vital role in who they've become and what they've accomplished.

It is indeed important to provide encouragement not only to the children who think outside the box, but also to the parents of these children. When your child pursues interests that differ from those of children in his or her age group, it can often be difficult to nurture the distinctive qualities. This book provides such parents and other motivated readers with different scenarios of children who thought differently while growing up, the obstacles they encountered, and how they got through it all to become the accomplished adults they are today. These personal narratives, authored by notable individuals who have changed or added to our world in some way, are inspirational, aiming to encourage and provide parents with the feeling of certainty and confidence regarding their child who thinks differently.

Through my work and my teaching, I have also seen that it is often the *intrinsic*, unique characteristics and passions that outside-the-box children possess that fuel their future success. I have become an advocate for such children, especially at the preschool level. I have learned that if a topic is interesting, meaningful, and relevant to the child it has optimum potential for educating and entertaining. When a parent, caregiver, teacher, or a child finds that special topic, there is no limit to what that child may accomplish. If a child's fascination is with dinosaurs, encourage that child to delve deeper into the world of dinosaurs. You may soon find that math, science, reading, art, writing, music, social skills, almost any discipline can be taught through a study of dinosaurs. By permitting young children to be themselves and follow their passions—be it dinosaurs or something else—parents and teachers are allowing their children to pursue their dreams, live up to their true potential, and become their best.

Part III, The Source Book: Exceptional Programs, Adventures, and Voyages for Your Child: Ages Youth to College, is a directory of programs divided by distinctive qualities and characteristics. These are often the very things that, with or without parental help, inspire a child to great accomplishments. This book provides the parent, caregiver, and teacher with helpful tools. There is a wealth of knowledge in these pages that allows you to unlock the unique qualities and characteristics in your child, helping each child realize his or her true potential. If your child is a strong debater or is fascinated by world politics, then the section entitled *Leader: Negotiator, Debater, Peacemaker* can provide you with some insight into the types of camps and programs that might work for your child. If your child is interested in humanity and helping the world, then the section entitled *Altruist: Community Servant, Healer, Teacher* might be of interest. *Kids Who Think Outside the Box* is a book that tells a parent that it is not only okay to have a kid who thinks differently, but that a child who is an individual thinker has many roads of possibility ahead of them.

My career goal, first as an educator in early childhood development and now as lead educational consultant for many highly successful properties of children's programming, has always been consistent: to relay a message that without fail includes the importance of encouraging the *individual self* within a child. When producing quality entertainment that is developmentally appropriate for the intended audience, I place this message first and foremost. The message of encouraging the *individual self* within a child is what *Kids Who Think Outside the Box* is all about. Through the poignant writings of thirty contributors, who themselves were kids who thought outside the box, you get a front row view of the importance of embracing your child's individual self.

Most importantly, I believe that this book will encourage you to look anew at your own "outside of the box" kid. With that second look, you will find what you always knew in your heart was there: your child is unique, distinctive, different, and certainly something special.

This is a must-read book for all parents and teachers. It is a book that will allow you to see how truly wonderful and unique your child or student is. Open these pages and discover the encouragement and strength you need to allow your child to realize their maximum potential. This book is your guide to fostering your child's individual self and helping your child achieve amazing accomplishments.

Mary Ann Dudko, Ph.D.

Dr. Dudko earned her doctorate in early childhood education and child development and has taught preschool, kindergarten, elementary school, and graduate level courses during the past 30 years. She is the Vice President of Content Development for *Barney & Friends®*, *Bob the Builder®*, *Thomas & Friends®*, *Angelina Ballerina®*, and all other properties produced by HIT Entertainment. She has also authored or coauthored more than 30 books for Barney Publishing.

PREFACE

K IDS WHO THINK OUTSIDE THE BOX is a point of reference for parents, teachers, and all who are fortunate enough to have or know a child who is unique in thought, spirit, and personality. The book motivates and inspires through the personal accounts of "living legends"—notably accomplished individuals who have contributed their stories to this book—who share with us the sources of motivation used to reach their personal pinnacle.

The book is comprised of three distinct parts. In the first section, we look at "who is the kid that thinks outside the box"; offer strategies for parents, teachers, and guidance counselors; and discuss the importance of embracing a child's differences. We then lay the essential groundwork for bringing out the most in a child who, one day, may be an eminent achiever.

The second part of the book consists of personally written contributions from world-renowned individuals describing what inspired them to reach their personal highpoint and present level of accomplishment. The insights and perspectives of these distinctive innovators and pioneers illustrate the limitless opportunities and possibilities that life has to offer.

The third part of the book is an information bank—a reference for identifying and locating unique programs for the exceptional child who has no interest in the cookie-cutter programs that appeal to the average child. I say it's a point of reference because it combines the characteristics of a typical reference book with insights essential to identifying the special programs that will contribute to your child's growth and enhance his or her potential.

Last, *Kids Who Think Outside the Box* is for my twelve-year-old son Morgen, the astronomer, rocket designer, and builder, who has taken our family to planets and destinations we never would have visited. He is *one* interesting kid, who "thinks outside the box."

Stephanie Lerner

ACKNOWLEDGMENTS

AS IT'S THE PEOPLE with you along the way who make the journey fulfilling, exciting, and worthwhile; I'd like to acknowledge my entire family. My mother always showed unconditional support and my father always told me to *go for it;* thank you. Harold and Paula Freund have been married for half of a century, and as parents they taught me that each day is important, each day is special, and each day should be valued. I have learned from them and the way they lived their lives.

I'd like to acknowledge and remember my grandmother, Matilda Levinsky, who was a female role model before it was fashionable. Her no-nonsense strength and loyalty to "her own," along with her indelible spirit showed me the way. My grandfather, Julius Levinsky, was our family's link to who we are. I live by the example they both set. It is through the lives of my grandparents that I find strength, wisdom, and insight.

Much gratitude goes to the people who have embraced this project from the beginning. To Lyudmila Bloch, a woman who makes her own accomplishments look seamless, thanks for the encouragement, optimism, and assistance. To every "living legend" and "eminent achiever" who contributed a narrative to the book, thank you for taking time out of your busy lives to write and express your thoughts and to share a little bit of what makes you the people you are today.

Kids Who Think Outside the Box is a tribute to children who have an innate sense of self and possess individuality: the talent and distinctiveness needed to reach for the stars. I acknowledge those significant educators in the lives of my children who recognize the importance of embracing children's differences and have walked that extra mile to guide them on their way to the finish line.

Special thanks to my husband who has persevered relentlessly on behalf of our family; it's always recognized. To Joe Checkler, the best and most efficient writer and participant a project could ever have. A very special thank you to Anita Gill, you did a fabulous job. Great research and writing . . . you will be quite a success at whatever you do. Larry Davidson, for the countless calls and stimulating discussions, you are officially appreciated.

Morgen, Chelsae, and Spencer, I say your names repeatedly every day, and yet when I think about it, I still can't believe you're mine. You are three distinct individuals with three different smiles, three special hearts, and three different outlooks on life—enjoy your journey. You'll do great!

Stephanie Lerner

INTRODUCTION

WHO ARE THE KIDS WHO
THINK OUTSIDE THE BOX?

It's twilight, soccer season, my older son, my eight year old is on the field, and he's the goalie. It's a practice game in the evening. The score is tied. The field is well lit, almost glowing, against the chilly November sky. This is what it is all about. I'm a soccer mom; he's a soccer kid. Oh my gosh . . . the ball is coming to him. I'm so glad I pushed him to all those practices. I know it wasn't easy for him, he wasn't that athletic, but I thought no pain, no gain.

"Morgen, you can do it honey, look alive, the ball is coming right to you," I yelled in a voice filled with support and hope for both him and me. Whew! He's in position, ready to get that ball. "What's going on," I thought to myself. He's looking at the sky, not the ball.

Maybe at eight years old he has his own strategy. "Morgen, look at the ball . . . look at the ball . . . look at the ball." I yelled as I clapped my hands, cheering him on. The ball was moving down the field, right toward my son the goalie. Morgen again looked up to the sky and not at the ball. Maybe at the age of eight he was spiritual and was praying to God for a win. With one last kick from the other team, the ball was coming directly at him. "Easy recovery," I thought to myself. Then to my horror, while my eight year old was engrossed in something celestial, the ball went right through his legs and the other side had scored a goal.

"What were you doing?" I yelled from the sidelines. With a gleam in his eye, he turned and looked at me as he pointed to the sky. "Look Mom, I think I spotted a double star." I wanted to cry. Not because we lost the game and not because he missed the goal. I wanted to cry because I was trying to make my wonderful, bright, scientific child something he was not and never could be. Now it was time for him to feel good about what he was about. From that day on, we didn't look back; we located programs and activities that utilized the intellect, insights, talents, and wisdom. We didn't stop at go, didn't push him to be something he was not, and once we knew we had a "kid who thought outside the box," our family hit the ground running.

Is the "kid who thinks outside the box" primarily a science whiz kid or math prodigy? Is he or she the kind of boy or girl hidden behind a thick set of glasses? No way! This child may or may not have a set of thick glasses, but this child has limitless potential and an intense focus in areas that are of interest to him or her. The "mainstream" kid is better rounded—"jacks of all trades"—which tends to work for parents and teachers, but, as you will see, mainstream kids also have "out-of-the-box" qualities.

For a variety of reasons, even the best-intentioned and most open-minded parent and teacher want their children to *fit in.* First and foremost, they believe, it is easier for the child, whom they dearly love, to have a "light-hearted" childhood with easy relationships. Sometimes that happens with a kid who thinks outside the box and sometimes it doesn't.

While contacting Tori Murden McClure, the first woman to cross the Atlantic Ocean by herself in a rowboat and the first women to reach the South Pole, I spoke with her husband briefly. I told him about the type of child I was writing about, and he hit the nail on the head when he described the kid who thinks outside the box as *prefocused.* I thought this description was perfect because this kind of kid either knows *who she is* and *what his interests are* at an early age, or, at least, they definitely know *who they are not*—certainly a unique attribute for a child, which clearly exhibits an innate strong sense of self.

Who are these kids who think outside the box? According to the 31 world eminent achievers, who contributed their stories to this book, they are children who have strong determination, love, and passion for their interests and relentlessly pursue their goals until their own personal level of success is reached.

The kid who thinks outside the box, can be Rod Gilbert, the Hall of Fame hockey player who was temporarily paralyzed and faced the possibility of having his legs amputated, yet overcame this obstacle to achieve his lifelong dream and became the all-time leading scorer on the New York Rangers Hockey team. This uniquely exceptional child can be Vinton Cerf, cofounder of the Internet, or Brian Martin, Olympic medal bronze and silver medal Olympic medal winner for luge in 1998 and 2002 (and going for the gold in 2006), or Mario Molina, Nobel Prize winner, who discovered the hole in the ozone layer of the Earth's atmosphere.

Our kid who thinks outside the box is not only the scientific child who will change the world through medical innovation, she is the kid we think of as a "super" intellectual. The out of the box child thinks uniquely when it comes to the pursuit of his or her goals.

Eighteen-year-old Rachael Scdoris, the athlete who overcame the many obstacles of blindness to become a top contender for the Iditarod, a grueling 1100 mile dog sled race, is a kid who thinks differently. Bob Hormats, vice-chairman of Goldman Sachs international, a man who is as comfortable and accomplished in the realm of public service as he is in the private sector, thinks differently. Mr. Hormats' current focus is on the advancement of business and financial innovation, worldwide, but before joining Goldman Sachs, he served as a senior staff member for international economic affairs on the National Security Council, and senior economic advisor to Dr. Henry Kissinger, General Brent Scowcroft, and Dr. Zbigniew Brzezinski.

I read the narrative contributed by Mike Mullane, a NASA astronaut, to my brother, who immediately commented that he wished he were more like Mike Mullane. I was flabbergasted. My brother, a plastic surgeon, was also a phenomenal athlete. Upon his graduation from high school, he was written up in one of the major newspapers in New York for his unique combination of academic and athletic attributes. His focus was always on becoming a doctor, and he worked hard in pursuit of his goal. He seemed to have little use for most kids. When you walked into his bedroom, the first thing you'd spot was his homemade sign that read, "no pain . . . no gain!" When I'd wake up a five o'clock in the morning, there he'd be at his desk working at some task essential to reaching his goals.

I said to my brother, "you are like that." "Maybe," he said quietly, "but I think I'm more thin-skinned than Mullane." I remembered years ago reading an entry in my brother's notebook that talked about the difficulty he had fitting in with other kids and not knowing what to do about it or how to handle it. My heart sunk; I felt so sorry for him but helpless. I immediately showed it to my mother, and she told me she'd take care of it. Later, he became a star swimmer and with it came much acclaim. I stopped worrying about him, but I realize now that life still wasn't easy for him.

When we need perspective raising our children, my mother pulls out her famous family story of the day Mrs. Berkowitz, my brother's second grade teacher, called to tell her that my brother was slow and needed special help. "I was going to pull him out of school and find a special school for him," she continues the story. "But your father, said to me, 'there is nothing the matter with this kid . . . we'll work with him,' and then the following year he had two fabulous teachers, and that was the beginning for your brother." Was it the teachers that changed my brother's experience? Was it that he was maturing? Was it that my parents approached him differently? Probably all of the above.

These kids may be prefocused, but they are still kids. They are sensitive, they need guidance, they are vulnerable, and they need to be accepted for who and what they are. As a parent, that's not always easy. We want the best for our kids and sometimes what we think is best may be missing the mark. A good teacher or role model can make a kid's year; an intuitive teacher, who can relate to an "out-of-the-box" kid, can make a child's life.

One of the more interesting phone calls I have received came from Barbara Levine, a former educator and a mom with a grown son who was an out-of-the-box kid. "He was different than other children, more difficult, not what I expected. I didn't know how to deal with him. I'm not quite sure if I was a good mother to him. I didn't understand him and you would think I would have and should have, I was a teacher," she continued in an emotional tone, "but I wanted a child who was the same as everyone else's child. If only had I known," she ended the call remorsefully. Michael is now an accomplished and successful technology entrepreneur.

Why am I writing this book? I'm writing this book because I am the mom of a son who thinks differently. I am the sister of a brother who was prefocused and motivated. I am a person who wishes that instead of working hard to be part of the group, to be popular and well accepted, someone had made me understand that there was true and unique value in identifying my differences. I wish someone told me that the process of appreciating my unique differences would inevitably be the key to my ultimate personal and professional success.

Do mainstream kids have out of the box potential? You bet! We work so hard at making sure our children fit in. We embrace our children's similarities and smooth out their differences when we should be accepting a child's differences and facilitating the expansion of these distinctive qualities that will inevitably "broaden their horizons" and enhance their futures. Raising a kid who thinks outside the box or locating the out of the box qualities of a mainstream child is hard work for a parent, but when all is said and done it's worth it.

This is evidenced by the stories told by our accomplished group of contributors, who, *for the most part*, led prefocused childhoods. Their passion and love for their talent or subject most times came early. For the most part, they were not "mainstream kids." Their narratives are poignant, inspirational, moving and enlightening.

Over the course of rearing my three children, I have focused their attention on interesting individuals, who have accomplished amazing things, as examples of what can be done. What excites and inspires me daily—and what I try to pass on to my children—is that there are so many groundbreaking brilliant people in the world, These men and women are not necessarily the people you read about in the press every day, and yet, on some level, they have significantly changed our lives and the world or met the challenges life has threw at them with flying colors.

Living legends and eminent achievers have inspired me throughout my career. Our culture and media tend to focus on the famous actress, rock star, or athlete when they tell "success stories." To me there is no greater success story than the creation of the Internet, there is not a more awe-inspiring story than Adam Riess' discovery that our universe is five billion years older than originally calculated and expanding, not contracting, as initially thought.

Success comes in all shapes and sizes as the stories of our "living legends" and "eminent achievers" amply illustrate. They did not possess a "cookie-cutter" blueprint to success. And just as there was not one winning road for them, there is no one particular road for any of us. Each child is an original; the only one of its kind on the planet with his or her own exceptional journey. Individuality is the key to achieving their personal best. I am hopeful that their stories will motivate parents and kids alike. Each story is different, each contributor is different, their writing styles are different, their visions are different, but the one thing that is the same is that they are all unique in thought, spirit, and personality.

Is there one or several similar factors that allowed our "eminent achievers" in their accomplishments? What is the key to the success of our contributors? Are there similarities in their support systems? Did they have a strong mother and a devoted father?

Each story is to be interpreted by you the reader, and you should draw your own conclusions. At times you'll recognize your own child or a child you know in a story, and at times you'll find yourself. The one thing I am sure of is that our contributors also had obstacles to overcome and that their success was a product of hard work, determination, and tapping in on their unique talent.

They participated in this book to pass along what they learned from their life's journey. They felt it important to pass along to parents, teachers and educators that however kids begin life, with support and acceptance, they can become the next great surgeon, inventor, Nobel Prize winner, police officer, Olympic champion, leader; that is, the best "individual" they can be. It's not easy. It never really is. But it can be done.

This next part of the book contains their stories; they are inspirational, tenacious, and, in some ways, they are just like you and me, and like our children. The narratives are written for both parents and children. The stories, which let us take a look into their individual journeys, say so much about life, determination, and commitment. Some are personal and revealing; others give us an important glimpse into the way our eminent achievers and living legends look at life. One thing that shines through is that each of them is unique in thought, spirit, and personality; each thinks outside the box and each has dedicated his or her life to personal excellence. I look up to each and every one of them. I have learned from all of them.

Kids Who Think Outside the Box is meant to be a "point of reference" for parents, teachers, and *all* who are fortunate enough to have or to know the child who is unique in thought, spirit, and personality. As much as I shy away from the word "cool," in this book I intend to demonstrate that it is cool to be smart, it is cool to be unique, it is cool to be an individual, it is cool to be different, and it is cool to see the world through innovation-colored glasses. That's the way Bill Gates started; that was Steven Spielberg's childhood reality.

Yes, it is easier for a parent and teacher to have and teach a mainstream kid. Although all kids are challenging, the mainstream child better fits the mold and is easier to teach. They fit into regular sized clothes, they follow the pack, the average curriculum suits them, and they just make life easy. Their intellectual parameters are predictable and defined. They are the norm, the same, and require little additional or innovative thought when teaching them. The kid who thinks outside the box is exciting, because there is a wealth of possibility and originality within that child. When that ability is tapped, you may discover, living under your roof, a future scientist, leader, or writer.

This book is for all of you who nurture a special child whose world revolves around *looking at the stars*, the child whose head and imagination is crammed with books about dinosaurs, fossils, and archaeology. It provides program alternatives for the child who is the *observer of life* and captures the experiences of others in his diary, the kid who may be the future writer or social commentator of our times, and the child who falls in love with the luge and may one day achieve the gold.

Through the personal accounts of dozens of such children, today's "living legends," world-renowned individuals who have made contributions in a variety of fields—from the arts to the sciences, you will be inspired by their stories of what motivated them to reach their personal pinnacles of success. Their stories illustrate that a childhood is a moment in time, leading to the path of limitless opportunities, achievements, and adventures.

Kids Who Think Outside the Box is comprised of three sections.

Part One identifies the characteristics of the kid who thinks outside the box. It illustrates the importance of this child within a group, commmunity, and family. This section emphasizes to parents, teachers, guidance counselors, and others the importance of acceptance and respect in regard to this child who is not the "cookie-cutter" kid. It then provides strategies and insights from experts to bring out your child's fullest potential—those magical qualities that are paramount to a child achieving his or her personal best.

The second part of the book, "Living Legends and Eminent Achievers," consists of 31 personal contributions from individuals who thought distinctively in their youth and because of their awe-inspiring individuality significantly succeeded in adulthood.

Almost every contribution in this section was specifically written for this book. In some cases it took two years to reach these notable persons because of their work commitments, painstaking travel schedules, and the thousands of participation requests they receive each year.

Once their personal commitment was made to this project, each of these pioneers and innovators felt it vital to share their unique beginnings and perspectives with parents and children, no matter how difficult and personal. Many of these stories are quite profound and often personally revealing, in order to exhibit that individuality, persistence, and a strong sense of self are imperative to a child's road to personal accomplishment.

Part Three is a directory of exceptional programs that exist for the kid who thinks outside the box. If your child's talent is leadership, it's never too early to recognize this attribute. If your child is an adventurer, there are programs for this kid who possesses the spirit of exploration. There are countless camps, voyages, and ventures that are exeptional and distinctive in every community. Our guide provides you with a place to begin.

In today's world, children who are driven by their own intellectual pursuits and gravitate toward different interests, activities, and hobbies, at times feel out of the social loop. This book will offer diverse alternatives to the child with limitless and unique intellect and talent.

Stephanie Lerner

Kids
who think
the outside
the box

Nurturing Your Unique Child

Do All Kids Have Out-of-the-Box Potential? You Bet They Do!

THINK DIFFERENT! This phrase makes for a strong, successful, and inspiring Apple Computer ad campaign, but, although much emphasis is placed on the importance of an individual being diverse in thought and spirit, parents and educators alike seem to fear a child who is an original, who may be out of step with the kid next door.

In most cases, our concern is for our child's well-being; we want our children to be well liked, to feel they're part of a team, and, dare I say it—popular. We justify these feelings by thinking that the mainstream kid integrates better into the community and therefore will interact more effectively, make a stronger contribution, and ultimately be more successful than the child who thinks as a unique individual. In many cases, mainstream kids do assimilate more smoothly and easily into social situations and their own personal neighborhoods, but often it is the children with out-of-the-box characteristics, who have the ability to make a significant and inspiring contribution to their community and the talent and vision to change the world in a positive way.

Out-of-the-box qualities and characteristics are the stepping stones that will help a child ultimately achieve his or her personal best; that will better enable him or her to reach for the stars. These distinctive attributes are driven by intellect, talent, a dynamic persona, and any other factor that elevates the child to a level above and/or outside the norm. These attributes make a child a vibrant exception to the masses.

An out-of-the-box kid can be that shy child who hasn't yet developed social skills, but has a highly sophisticated comprehension of and interest in the universe. Peers might call this child a "geek" or "nerd" but in twenty years that child might be an innovator in space exploration. Another might be overly outgoing, a well-liked child who possesses an uncharacteristic level of maturity and compassion and a highly developed social conscience. You feel that this child could reinvent the "Peace Corps" by the ripe old age of seven. This is our future leader, writer, and commentator.

Any child can have out-of-the-box traits. Parents, teachers, counselors, and significant educators need to identify these qualities, work with the child to pursue and develop the characteristics at which he or she is adept, preserve the child's individuality, and help that child integrate into the group, the classroom, and community.

This element of distinctiveness should be encouraged in all kids. Mainstream children are often rewarded for their sameness, which then becomes the key to who they are. Yet, they too may have wonderfully unique attributes that will be enhanced only if nurtured and explored. As a rule, up until the time they are ready to apply for college, mainstream kids are held up as the group to emulate and deemed "most likely to succeed."

Then it's time for college, and the qualities that have successfully taken a child through high school are not enough. A little more is needed: more individuality, more breadth, and more depth. Suddenly, those wonderful interests that set an out-of-the-box kid apart from the mainstream are now in demand.

In interviews, several directors of admissions from well-known universities around the country explained that three elements are considered crucial for admission:

- The candidate should clearly demonstrate high quality; an all-round balanced person who has successfully developed his or her talent. Although many kids possess stellar academic records, the applicant who has identified his or her special abilities, worked on them, built on them, and utilized them is the one who meets the tangible and intangible talent criteria that the school is seeking.
- The school also assesses "how well the candidate does the things he/she loves." This is an extension of the first point, and the next step in the process. Once the child has discovered "uniqueness of self," what he or she does with that raw talent becomes the measure of success. Of course, the directors didn't expect an applicant's résumé to read like that of a superstar in the field, but they were looking for personal accomplishment that was individual and was pursued since childhood.
- The candidate should have as much potential to develop future ability as was demonstrated in the past. A prospective student is judged on how well the college feels he or she will "develop those abilities for the benefit of themselves, the workforce, and society."

The directors also made it clear that not every school is right for every child and emphasized that careful attention should be paid to locating the setting that will bring out the best in each student. An admissions professional from Harvard advised parents to know their child and to give that child a lot space to figure out what he or she loves to do and suggested that teachers and counselors, to the extent possible, must be aware of each child as an individual.

The question and challenge is how to positively nurture a child's unique qualities and distinctive characteristics at the same time as the child is integrated into an educational and social environment, so that childhood can be a magical time of growth, wonder, and development.

Deborah Hardy, former president of the New York State School Counselor Association (NYSSCA) and a school counselor in Irvington, New York, also provided valuable insight into *what* and *who* is important to the success of a child's total educational experience. "Working with parents, teachers, kids, and administrators in the process of the *total* education of a child is integral to a positive outcome. Unlike other fields, I have learned that all of us who are active in the teaching process have to be a jack-of-all trades and 'an expert at all.'" Based on her years of experience, she offered some practical advice to teachers, administrators, and parents:

> **Teachers:** As early as kindergarten, it is important to incorporate your student's experiences into the classroom. Learning goes beyond the classroom environment and by asking students to share outside activities, endeavors, and encounters with others, you enhance the child's position within the group. You also add to the diversity and collective self-esteem of the classroom.
>
> Memory-based tests should not be the only way to assess academic and classroom success, especially in the lower and middle school years. Encourage a variety of assessments. Let students show their talents and interests through portfolios, drawings, or music. She recommends

incorporating discussions on topics relevant to the material and incorporating problem solving, analysis, and the discovery of new ideas and concepts into the classroom.

It's essential that teachers get to know their students. Learning who these children are and integrating their special qualities into the personality and fabric of the classroom, enhances the individual's as well as the group's learning experience.

Teachers also need time to share with one another their ideas for enhancing the student's learning and interests. It also gives them perspective, strategies, and new ideas.

Administrators: Teachers need a strong educational and visionary plan. Too often administrators forget that their work affects the student. Administrators must set the vision and then frequently communicate with the teachers to ensure they are working well together; sometimes ideas work in theory, but not in practice. It's also a good idea to work with the school counselor to establish a class time to get student feedback on problem solving, curriculum discussion, interests, and the development of activities and groups that may not be present at the school.

Parents: It is the parent's job to raise strong, independent children with a definite sense of self. You are there to guide and educate them. Parents who are overprotective limit what works for their children.

Trust is a major factor. Parents must trust their children, themselves, and their parenting values. This is paramount in the development of the solid parenting skills and strategies needed to raise a well-balanced child.

Children react well to approval, which, in many cases, they take to mean love. It's important for parents to listen to their children. Approval is important to all of us.

Children's behavior is affected by their environment. Although grades are important, approval should also be based on how a child overcomes obstacles and meets challenges.

As Deborah Hardy implies, in addition to the parent, the teacher has the most important role in educating and building the self-esteem of a child. Encouraging individuality within the established constraints of a classroom while challenging the child, is pivotal. Just as the out-of-the-box children should be encouraged to pursue their significant talents within the framework of the classroom, so too should mainstream children be supported in the pursuit of their unique traits. This should be a time of self-exploration for all children.

How does a teacher achieve the proper balance? How does a teacher take a "diamond in the rough," recognize and encourage differences, and still successfully integrate that child into the classroom? It is a challenging job, and it takes the right personality, intuition, training, and teaching skills to effectively master this undertaking.

Gail McGoogan, Disney Elementary Teacher of the Year, 2003 (American Teacher Award) clearly has a strategy that is innovative, inspiring, and tailor made for her unique students. In my interview with Ms. McGoogan, she was straightforward and direct:

> For all my special students who quietly search for a means of expression, our learning environment must expand beyond the four walls of a classroom; it must encompass life's experiences. For example, if students need to understand what the area in which they live was like in the days of early settlers when all they see now are roads and attractions, *become* an early settler and canoe on a secluded creek. Design and build a pioneer cabin and sleep out

under the stars. Sing and dance and share stories around a campfire. If a child needs to connect to society through service, restore yards for needy families. Refurbish a lakefront and share it with the community. Somewhere through these real life experiences a spark will be lit that, in time, will light the way for those quiet, deep thinkers who have yet to glow on their own.

I asked her if the teacher who works hard to promote the distinctiveness of each child requires a less disciplined environment within which to work. She replied, "I am not so certain that the approach to teaching is 'out of the box,' but rather using the stability of the box and stretching it to its utmost. I do know that all students learn better when they understand the meaning and purpose of what they are learning." I think of McGoogan's philosophy as *structure plus:* a structured environment that goes hand in hand with the tailor-made innovative teaching methods and approaches necessary to reach all students. Some of my children's most inspiring teachers are those who expected great things from them as students and as people.

Another vitally important characteristic is fairness. Most people have one teacher who changed their lives in some significant way. Ms. Carlino, my algebra teacher, changed mine. She maintained her position of authority in a matter-of-fact way. In the early 1970s, when structure was a concept that was rapidly being abandoned, Ms. Carlino started her class each day with a morning greeting. She would face us and pertly say, "Good morning class," and we would all respond, "Good morning Ms. Carlino," and then she would instruct us to be seated. We laughed and snickered the first day, but then we got it. The greeting became second nature, and when it was done, we knew that math class had begun.

Ms. Carlino was also fair. The point was for all of us, with very different aptitudes, to learn algebra. That was Ms. Carlino's expectation. If you didn't get it in class, she had regularly scheduled after school study classes—no one had to ask for help. The classes were there, and no child was singled out for not knowing the material. Ms. Carlino was there at 3:10 PM, right after school, in our math room ready to coach whoever showed up. No question was considered dim.

Parents have so much to learn. Each of my three children is different and, as a result, I am a different parent to each. I look at the world differently for each of them because through their eyes the world is different. As an adult who is in the "parenting business," I look at their world through my eyes as well; with my values, perceptions, and innate child development strategies and tools. How do I guide them in their optimal direction, the one that suits them best? How do I know which teacher is best for them, and how do I work best with the school counselor? How can I direct them down a path that enables them to be whole and strong, one that will develop their sense of confidence and self? I know it's by listening to my children, gaining strength from my values and beliefs, and learning through the experience of others, along with a strong dose of parental self-confidence. Most times that is easier said than done.

PART TWO

Living Legends and Eminent Achievers

THEIR STORIES

O NE OF MY most special possessions is a photograph of my eldest son and daughter. It's 6×9 inches and not even framed—one of things I just haven't gotten to—but I always have it near at hand to remind me of my responsibility to these innocent, beautiful, complex, challenging, and different children I have brought into the world. The photograph was not posed, and it absolutely didn't catch them at their "cheesecake" best, but it did capture the beautiful innocence in their eyes—the innocence that only a child can possess. I look at this picture often when child rearing becomes challenging because it reminds me that whatever difficulty they are experiencing, my job is to help guide them through it.

What better examples can we give our children than the opportunity to learn through the lives of others? In today's world, kids are constantly exposed to the "dark side," and, with all due respect to Darth Vader, I prefer to teach my children from the best in life.

The stories you are about to read were written by "living legends" and "eminent achievers." Each describes how he or she reached the height of success. Each has accomplished great things; each has overcome obstacles; and, most importantly, each has never given up. Superstardom is not easy to achieve in any field, but these people have done it.

As you'll see, these stories are inspirational because they illustrate each person's tenacity and dedication to excellence. At the same time, we learn that superstars are people just like you and me, and just like our children. I look up to each and every one of them. I have learned from all of them. I think you will, too.

THE ARTISTS

Spike Lee
Filmmaker, Actor, Author, Teacher

A s I spoke with Spike Lee, I immediately understood why he accomplished what he set out to do with his life. As a professor and artistic director at New York University's graduate film program, he begins his course "directing strategies" by explaining that he doesn't accept excuses when it comes to completing a project. Of all people, he should know what it takes. It is now part of show business lore that he maxed out every credit card in his possession and tapped every possible source of funds to produce his first film, *She's Gotta Have It*, which not only earned him the prestigious "New Generation Award" but set him at the forefront of the Black New Wave in American cinema. Today, Lee is one of Hollywood's most important and influential filmmakers with critically acclaimed films, such as *Malcolm X*, *Clockers*, and *Do the Right Thing*.

Born in Atlanta, Georgia and raised in Brooklyn, New York; Mr. Lee returned to Atlanta to attend Morehouse College.

After graduation, he continued his education at New York University's Tisch School of the Arts in Manhattan, where he received his Master of Fine Arts Degree in film production.

Lee's reputation is not without controversy. His movies are sometimes criticized for not representing the most positive side of the black experience or of the relationships between blacks and whites. Nevertheless, he holds true to his vision and his art. He started off as a maverick, doing what he loves, and, no doubt, he will continue to bring his unique message and vision to his movies.

When it comes to his own life, his priorities are his family, his kids, and his art. Already focused as a child, he has certainly remained focused as an adult. He remains an out-of-the-box thinker and is a noteworthy example of a creative individual who circumvented the traditional route to success, followed his dreams, and worked hard to achieve his personal best.

Spike Lee
A Strong Sense of Self

It's a parent's job to expose their kids to the world around them and what it offers, kids don't know what they can do unless they are exposed to it.

I owe all my success to my parents and grandparents, because they instilled in me a sense of confidence. Even before I became a filmmaker, or wanted to become a filmmaker, they worked hard to provide me with a sense of self that has stayed with me in whatever I do or undertake.

Source: Printed with the permission from Shelton J. "Spike" Lee, Writer, Director Producer.

We grew up in a very artistic family. My siblings and I were exposed to the arts at a very young age. We weren't discouraged from the arts because it wasn't a guaranteed future, and I never heard my parents say not to try something because there wasn't money in it or it wasn't a pursuit that they would have chosen for themselves or for us. If we enjoyed and pursued our interest, our parents and grandparents supported it.

Too often parents kill their kid's dreams. I'm not saying that parents do this on purpose; they want to protect their children. They don't want their children to go through the heartache and the hardships that they experienced. They want their children to be very productive and not worry about money, so they guide them into a profession where they are guaranteed to get a check every week. But that might not be what the kid wants to do, or is good at, or will be happy at.

It's a parent's job to expose their kids to the world around them and what it offers. Kids don't know what they can do unless they are exposed to it. They might have some extraordinary gift, but if they don't know what's out there and available to them, whatever that gift is, it unfortunately just languishes. That's why my family has played such a pivotal role in my accomplishment, and I appreciate the family that I had.

My turning point was in 1977. I was 20 years old, finishing my sophomore year at Morehouse College in Atlanta, Georgia. Before coming home to New York City, my adviser told me I really had to think about declaring a major. I really had no idea what I want to go into or what classes I wanted to take when I got to college, so I took and exhausted all my electives first. Well, I was now done with my electives and I had to focus on my major.

When I got home to New York City, it was during the summer of 1977. That was a famous summer; New York City was in dire financial straits, there was no money and there were no jobs. That previous Christmas, I had gotten a "Super 8" camera, so I spent the whole vacation running around with that camera, during that illustrious summer. Now of course that was the summer of David Berkowitz, the Son of Sam, and of a massive blackout. It also was the first summer of Disco in New York City, the dance was the "Hustle," and in many neighborhoods, you had block parties with D.J.s hooking up their speakers and turntables to the street lamps. So, it was a very exciting summer.

I made a film about that summer, a Super 8 film, called, *Last Hustle in Brooklyn*, which was my first film ever. It's ironic that many years later, I was able to go back and revisit that amazing summer of 1977 in a film called, *Summer of Sam*. So after this personally groundbreaking summer for me artistically, when I went back to school that fall and had to declare a major, I knew that filmmaking was what I really wanted to do.

Although I know my success is a result of the self-confidence my parents gave me, I can't overlook some great teachers who saw my potential. One teacher I had, who at the time was ruthless on my grammar and punctuation, was an English teacher by the name of Dr. Delores Stevens. She saw that I had some talent and just "stayed on me," so I would stay with it. She would mark my papers in red ink and at times it "looked as if someone had slit their wrists" on them. But she wanted me to be my personal best and care about my work and English. I cared. I didn't like it at the time, but now I see that she did me a great service, by not just letting me slide and get by.

As a child, I was kind of quiet, close to my siblings, but we would fight, and I always loved sports. In sports I could be myself. I was very vocal when I was playing sports. I wasn't the best player, but always the one with the biggest mouth—

the spunkiest you might say. What was great about sports was not only that I could be myself and was driven by my interest, but I was also able to use that drive, in different directions and areas of my life, and eventually direct it into my art.

To be an independent filmmaker you have to be relentless. I have taken the same attributes that make athletes not give up and keep going when the score is 100 to nothing, and have applied it do my profession. I won't quit. I think that's what you need to be when you are an independent filmmaker because things aren't set up for you to succeed. It's just rough. There were occasions when I did a couple of film projects that I had to abort—that blew up in my face—which had me seriously thinking about whether I should quit, but at the end of the day I said "I'm not a quitter" and I didn't quit.

My dream, for the future is to have my kids grow up healthy and strong with knowledge of self, great self-worth, and self-esteem because parents can't be with their kids 24/7. I feel sorry for kids today; they have to grow up much sooner, with a whole lot more stuff than what we had to grow up—sexual awareness, drugs. The things kids know and deal with today, I wasn't aware of until I was much older. Twelve year olds want to be eighteen year olds. I can't blame the kids. There is a lot pressure and they see what's out there in the media. So I feel it's my role as a parent to be tough and guide my children so that they have the knowledge and wisdom to make the right decisions.

I'm a disciplinarian as a dad. I am more of a disciplinarian than my father was. Whatever we wanted to do was cool with my father. He wanted his children to grow with total freedom —that's one philosophy, but that's not mine. My mother was forced into becoming the disciplinarian, because my father wouldn't do it. That wasn't fair to my mother, because kids grow up loving the parent who is more lenient. My mother wanted me to succeed; she was always on me. My mother really pushed. Her determination is with me and has stayed with me.

You always hear about fathers and sons in relation to sports, but I am careful not to leave my daughter out. My son plays soccer and just recently my daughter decided that she wants to play too, which is great. I try to be equal, I had to learn to do that, my wife Tania has been great in reminding me.

My parents were interesting people; my father is a jazz musician and my mother, who passed away, taught art history and African American literature. I come from an artistic educational background. My father and grandfather went to Morehouse and my mother and grandmother went to Spellman, which historically are the two top black schools. They set a standard through their example.

My parents both taught and through them, I know how important it is to teach. I love teaching. I'm in the film industry now, and I can take what I am doing at that very moment to the class and pass it on to future filmmakers. They can learn from me as I learned from my parents and teachers. I'm tough on the kids. I don't let them become lazy. Things are not instantaneous; there has to be hard work, elbow grease, and a kid needs "get up and go" to be successful. So I'm always on them, just as those people who cared about me were always on me. I try to pass along to them a work ethic. You can't just preach to them, so daily I try to set an example. That's what was illustrated to me by my parents and teachers, and I try to pass it along.

While growing up, when I looked outside my family, my role models were athletes and, of course, also Dr. King and Malcolm X, who were strong black leaders, but I also admired Jackie Robinson and Joe Lewis. They not only changed the landscape of sports, but the landscape of America.

Paul McCartney
Musician, Composer, Performer, Writer, Producer

R ewind the clock to a time before the Beatles were considered classic—when they were considered cutting
edge, when their hairstyles, dress, and attitude were considered radical. As with most of my generation, I am a Beatles
fan, perhaps the ultimate Beatles fan. Although I had not yet
entered my teens in the 1960s, the message that the Beatles
communicated through their music was woven into the fabric of my life.

I asked Paul McCartney to participate in *Kids Who Think
Outside the Box* because of his individuality, strength of conviction, and confidence in his art—his music and his message
were revolutionary at the time.

Paul McCartney was born on June 18, 1942, in Liverpool,
England. McCartney was the bass guitarist and vocalist for
the Beatles and a partner in a legendary songwriting team
with John Lennon. Together, they blazed a unique trail that
still influences all music. It communicated the message of a
changing time, without being deterred by those who resisted
those changes.

When we asked Sir Paul for some words of advice to pass
along to kids, he gave the advice he always gives—and has
heeded in his own life—which is a famous quotation from
Hamlet, "To thine own self be true." It sounds simple, almost
too ordinary, but on reflection you can see that that's the way
he has lived his life and made his music.

In the thirty years since the Beatles broke up, first with
Wings and then as a solo artist, he has continued breaking
down barriers and remains an influence on the sound of music
around the globe.

Paul McCartney
The Positive Power of Love

We were saying good, positive things. We were saying "all you need is love" or "there will be an answer, let it be."

One of the things that was cool about the Beatles, and something I'm very proud of, is what we said in the songs. We were saying good, positive things. We were saying "all you need is love" or "there will be an answer, let it be" or "it's a fool who plays it cool and makes his world a little colder." All of these messages were good messages; they weren't anthems of rebelliousness, we weren't saying, "C'mon kids, hate your parents"

The point is that we could have made those bad, hateful statements because the Beatles had power. But we didn't abuse that power, we tried to use what influence we had in our songs for the good; like speaking up for peace and love. We could have gone off in another direction and not have majored on the love thing; but that—the love thing—was important to us and it still is important.

I think if there is any sort of residue of love for the Beatles it's because we were very honest and because we spread that loving, genuine vibe. I still think that's right; that's really still all you need—love—that is all there is. If you look at some families these days, there seem to be a lot of problems because there isn't enough of that, that love. Kids are like baby animals; they imitate their parents; that's how they learn. So if you've got kids seeing their parents argue or fight, that's what they are going to learn.

But I believe that in these times, it's good that our message still remains as a very positive, loving message, and that there is hope that people will listen to it.

Source: Printed with permission from Paul McCartney.

Philippe Rousselot
Cinematographer, Artist, Filmmaker

To this day, Philippe Rousselot is still sensitive to the obstacles facing the independent, bright child, who is not the mainstream kid. In my first conversation with him, I was unaware of his "childhood reality," one of the few Jewish children living in a town in post-World War II France. As a result of this reality, his childhood was filled with loneliness and isolation, but he learned to embrace this loneliness and make it a part of who he is and who he has become.

His career is admirable. He began as an assistant to famed cinematographer Nestor Almendros on Eric Rohmer-directed films of the late 1960s and early 1970s. On his own, he lensed several of the nostalgic films of director Diane Kurys (*Peppermint, Soda, Cocktail Molotov*). For his versatile camerawork on the film *Diva*, he won the first of his César awards (the French Oscar). It was noted that the film was dependent on Rousselot's chic visuals.

His second César in 1986 was for the realistically stylish film *Thérèse*, and it was at about this time that he began venturing into English-language cinema with *Hope and Glory* (1987), *Dangerous Liaisons* (1988), and *Henry and June* (1991), for which he earned Oscar nominations. With *A River Runs Through It* (1992), he finally won the Oscar, and two years later, he won his third César for his camera work for *La Reine.*

Although Rousselot is an acclaimed cinematographer and his career has been a steady ascent, it is his childhood story that tells you what you really need to know about the person he has become.

Philippe Rousselot
Be Proud of Being Different

Cherish your independence even if it sometimes makes you feel lonely.

I was raised in a small, dull, unattractive village in the east of France, a village in the midst of being hastily rebuilt after World War II. The population consisted of hard-working farmers coping with incoming mechanization and easy credit that would soon provoke their disappearance and steel workers who mined steel at a time when that industry was running out of prosperity. Kids went to school only because they had to . . . knowing that family protocol would soon force them to take over the small family farm or join the workforce in the steel mill. My parents were probably the only people in the village who owned and read books, and they read with passion. They were also the only ones not to go to church.

As God did not exist in our house, one had to set his values on his own, which required much more attention and work than following any preset rules. And one had better get it right. Ethics were not something to be taken lightly in my family. Not being Catholic in a world that knew nothing else, separated me from other kids in a very definitive way. I could not join the local Boy Scouts (this would have required attending church), was not invited to the numerous religious events and their gargantuan banquets, and never knew about mass, wine tasting, or all those practical jokes altar boys bragged about at school. The church, which was located at the center of the village, was an ominous building, which I feared as mysterious and demonic until years later when I

Source: Printed with permission from Philippe Rousselot, cinematographer.

befriended the priest and went in to teach myself to play the pipe organ.

Not attending mass on Sunday morning and Vespers in the afternoon and Bible class on Thursday meant I had a lot of time to kill and no friends to pass it with. So I had time to read. From Tolstoy to Gogol to Dostoyevsky, I read my mother's entire collection of Russian literature.

Having a mother who came from such a remote land as Russia would sometime provoke hostility and I did not even dare say she was Jewish, something unheard of in the village. It was right after World War II, and the fears that were prominent during the war still loomed strongly in everyone's head. Being Jewish was a bit of news one concealed, by habit, to ensure mortal survival.

Very soon I felt different from other kids and started keeping my thoughts and my readings for myself, instinctively knowing it was not right to howl with the pack and follow leaders. I wasn't into admiring the strongest and joining the mob no matter what face it used to disguise itself. My not being exactly what other kids wanted me to be often led to fights; bruises, cracked lips and split eyebrows, especially since I was usually the smallest of the class and the most inept at displaying physical force.

But let me tell you what led me to the job I am doing now. I was eleven years old when my parents sent me unaccompanied to a winter camp in the Alps. At the time, these things were not organized for kids the way they are now. A woman was supposed to chaperone me to my destination, but as soon as we boarded the train, she disappeared with some boyfriend, never to be seen again. During the long night spent in the train I wasn't sure if I was on the correct train or if it was going in the right direction. I was the only kid in the train and no one seemed to be concerned by that. In post WW II Europe, people took very little note to most things that were not of major consequence.

When I got to the camp, I found myself a most unwelcome person, with hardly a place to sleep in, no ski equipment and no one to befriend. I remember this as a place engulfed in constant darkness, where I wandered from one building to another aimlessly, hiding my tears and my shame at wasting a precious and so long-awaited vacation.

Then another kind of darkness saved my days. In the camp, I discovered a little film club where 16 mm prints of film classics were shown each night. Every evening I hid myself in the obscurity of the screening room only to face, when the lights came on, incredulous adults who could not understand the presence of a kid and his interest in their supposedly highly intellectual debate that followed each projection.

But in the anonymity of the dark screening room, I discovered extraordinary treasures: the black-and-white expressionist shadows of the *Golem and Caligary, Doctor Mabuse* and Murnau's *Dracula*, the masterpiece of the postwar neo-realism Italian cinema. I saw *The Night of the Hunter* and other great American classics. But what transformed me were films by Cocteau like *Le Testament d'Orphée, Le Sang d'un Poête* and the unparalleled *Beauty and the Beast*. Seeing *Beauty and the Beast*, with its images inspired by Vermeer (my favorite painter at the time), made me aware, for the first time, of the presence of a person behind the camera. And although I knew nothing at the time of the cinematographer Henri Alekan, or what being a cinematographer was like, I wanted to be that person.

At the end of the camp, I had done very little skiing, but knew what I would do in life. I wanted to make images. It was not a question of career, of money, not even of way of life.

There were images somewhere in a remote part of my mind that I needed to bring onto the screen.

If I were so bold as to give any advice, I would say this: never be ashamed of your differences or the thoughts that come to you. Cherish your independence even if it sometimes makes you feel lonely. Be happy in and with your solitude, for only in solitude will you find creativity. And whenever you see a work of art, a statue or a structure that interests you, take a few steps back and a few steps in all directions and find another point of view, your point of view.

John Nels Hatleberg
Artist, Designer

When I first met with John Nels Hatleberg, I wasn't quite sure if I was meeting a scientist, artist, technician, or entrepreneur. On entering his home art studio, I was struck by the ceramic floors, which he designed, as well as the unusual works of art made from a variety of pearls and precious gems. Our conversation, on the other hand, was laced with the technical and scientific information essential to the work of the world's most famous diamond cutter. He seemed so scientific and exact, attributes important to a gem cutter and designer, with the eye of an artist and the sense of a businessman.

John Hatleberg is known primarily as a conceptual artist who creates, among other things, exact replicas of famous diamonds. He has been invited by DeBeers, the Smithsonian Institution, the British Museum of Natural History, the South African government, and Dresden Vaults to work with their diamonds. Prominent jewelers have also enlisted his talents, including Robert Mouawad, Harry Winston, Cartier, and Thomas Farber. He has consulted with officials at Tower of London on the Kohinoor diamond in the permanent display, "Crowns and Diamonds," with Christie's auction house for the third edition of the book, *Famous Diamonds*, and on the landmark "Diamantes" exhibition in Paris.

John Nels Hatleberg
Security, Patience, Perseverance

There were not a lot of people able to tell me how to get here.
I struggled for years.

By age ten it was obvious that the piano lessons were not going to work. I have incredible parents, and they recognized that out of nowhere I had a passion for gems. It was unbelievably intuitive of them. How fortunate for me that they found and signed me up for a gem-cutting course at an adult education program in the basement of a suburban Maryland recreation center. It was me and a bunch of retirees cutting *agate cabochons* underground. It was the best of times.

When the course was over we signed me up again. While I was still in elementary school my parents found an elderly man in our community who introduced me to the pinnacle of "the art"—how to facet gems. Mostly though, Joe Touchette taught me about patience. I apprenticed with him on Saturday mornings until I left for college. While learning about gems with Joe, I also interned at the Smithsonian, which enhanced my quest and inevitably seasoned me to that precious world.

During college my faceting machine stayed with me, but I never turned it on. I was taking in the freedom of school and subconsciously searching for a way to link the interests that preceded even my early attraction to gems, *art* and *magic*, to the jewels themselves.

My pursuit of gems and art became an innate part of my being—both profound and spiritual. I guess I could have been

---

Source: Printed with permission from John Nels Hatleberg.

moved by sports—I loved to water ski and I unicycled so much that some people thought I didn't know how to walk. I could have been moved by religion or politics; but I chose art. I had the personality to be seized by this pursuit in a relentless manner.

My quest to master the *art and science* of conceptual gem artistry grew and continued. My life was committed to not only being the best at it, but also bringing it to the next possible level. This brought me back to the Smithsonian a few summers after I completed graduate school. It was at this time that I was afforded a pivotal and career altering experience by John White, the Smithsonian's gem curator.

It was almost as if I were reading a wonderful novel and I was a character in the book. The excitement of the story was building and the magical turning point was finally in reach. The story read like this:

> The Hope Diamond was taken from its vault and transferred to a darkened room. For several moments, John White, the Smithsonian gem curator, helped me charge this historical, rare and world-famous diamond with short wave light. In the darkness, the largest blue diamond in the world turned red and glowed like a coal, muted like a dying ember. The only light in the room came from the stone itself. This most famous of diamonds, steeped in centuries of intrigue and allure and of the highest cultural and historical rarity, was *phosphorescing* red. It seemed possessed.

Seeing this electrifying transformation irrevocably altered the art that has since emerged from me. I became aware that gems, which often serve as meaningful yet conventional symbols in our lives, have the potential to show us to ourselves, reveal aspects of our personalities and lives.

Artists are always remaking the same piece. I have probably spent the last twenty years attempting to create objects with a transcendence akin to that which emanates from engagement rings. They are a perfect package. This has led me to an unprecedented diversity in my work with jewels. I have vaporized diamonds to create diamond air, lasered pure gold tattoos, made mirrors of meteorites, sandwiched holograms in gems, and found a pearl that appears so uncannily to be a heart that people have sensed it beating.

For the last 15 years I have also had the honor of working with the world's most famous diamonds. I am primarily known for this work. When given complete access to a famous diamond, I can facet a replica that is visually indistinguishable from the original. It is shocking to compare the two jewels side by side. At times they incite awe.

The Hope-Centenary, Dresden Green, Eureka, Excelsior, Shah Jahan Table Cut, Guinea Star, McLean/Duchess of Windsor, Oppenheimer, Portuguese, B.1ueHeart, Millennium Star, Victoria Transvaal, Incomparable and other diamonds have been entrusted to my care. What is it like to work with these jewels? It is a transporting experience. The diamonds are so powerful, so beautiful, so rare, valuable, and seductive.

Some people say that I have worked on more famous diamonds than anyone else in history. In part due to technological advances, it is true that I am the only one in the world that has taken the creation of replicas to the realm of an exacting art form. There were not a lot of people able to tell me how to get here. I struggled for years.

In this narrative, I have suggested how I have pursued singular and potent jewels, how I am affected by them, and how I am able to transfer that inspiration to what I do. Of primary importance growing up was my feeling secure in my parents' love. They encouraged me to explore. My parents told me they would believe in me as long as I believed in myself. This security and my patience to follow a muse seem to insure my path.

This year I will be shown a new diamond recently wrenched from the earth in Africa, a diamond that is so vividly colored, so pure, so big, and so brilliant that when I look into it I expect I will see all the way to Pluto. I hope your travels in life take you far as well.

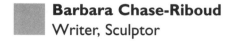

Barbara Chase-Riboud
Writer, Sculptor

Barbara Chase-Riboud is a trailblazing artist and writer. Born in 1929, she grew up in a middle-class black neighborhood near downtown Philadelphia. Her grandmother, the head of the household, was determined that Chase-Riboud should have the same well-rounded education available to any child in America and insisted that she take art and dance classes. Chase-Riboud's parents both possessed artistic talent. Her father was rejected from architecture school because of his color and abandoned painting to run the family's construction business, while her mother discovered her ability as a fiber artist only in retirement.

Chase-Riboud began her formal art studies at the age of seven at the Fletcher Art Memorial School and the Philadelphia Museum of Art, where it became evident that she was a prodigy. Although she was the only black child in her classes, she never felt out of place. She continued her training at the Philadelphia High School for Girls, received a BFA at the Tyler School of Art and Design, and went to the American Academy in Rome on a John Hay Whitney Fellowship. On her return, she attended Yale University on scholarship.

Chase-Riboud has achieved success in a wide variety of artistic areas. She was invited to the People's Republic of China, where she met with Chou en Lai and was invited to a state dinner with Mao Zedong. She wrote the "Chinese" poems after that visit. She went on to exhibit her memorial sculpture to *Malcolm X* at the Massachusetts Institute of Technology and began writing a novel, *Sally Hemings*, which was later acquired and edited by Jacqueline Kennedy Onassis. The novel, received international acclaim and won her the J.H. Kafka prize for a novel written by an American woman. She also was commissioned by the U.S. General Services

Department in 1995 to produce the African Burial Ground Memorial on Foley Square in New York City.

Barbara Chase-Riboud's new historical novel, *Hottentot Venus*, was published in 2003. It was awarded the American Library Association's best fiction prize in 2004.

Barbara Chase-Riboud
Never Be Afraid

Making things look easy is a matter of politeness. . . . Letting people know that you are carrying a burden is a third world attitude towards life. . . .

Can a five-year experience be a life-defining experience? Like the "Princess and the Pea" fairy tale, as a child I refused to sleep under the weight of bedcovers, and so my mother invented flannel pajamas that covered me from head to toe and allowed me to sleep uncovered. Once, when my aunt baby-sat for me, she left the window open and then insisted on drawing the covers up around my neck. Each time she did so, I would kick them off, stating in all truth that, "my mother doesn't cover me up."

"Nonsense," insisted my aunt, "the window's open, and you'll catch your death of cold. "I will not be responsible" and, as she left the room, she pulled the covers up again and turned off the lights. The third time I kicked the covers off and she pulled them up again, I sat up in my bed and punched her in the nose. "I told you that my mother doesn't cover me up," I said. From that day on I was "Miss My Mother Doesn't Cover Me Up."

Source: ©Barbara Chase-Riboud.

My five year-old outrage that truth, as I saw it, was not being respected turned my tiny fists into engines of mass destruction. This passion for truth and telling it as it is has served me well throughout a double career of searching for truth in beauty and beautifully sculpted objects and pursuing truth in narrative and history.

I remember as an 11-year-old poet, I was accused of copying a poem I had written all about autumn leaves and death and was commanded by my teacher to stand up in front of the whole class and "confess." When I refused to admit something I hadn't done, I was sent to the principal's office and when I again refused to confess my "crime," my mother was sent for, with the threat of suspending me from school. As my mother had actually witnessed me writing my poem on the edge of the dining room table, she declared that I would never set foot in that school again. And I never did. It was my mother who took me out of middle school and enrolled me in high school, but it was my grandmother who comforted me. "Never be afraid," she said, "they can't take what's in your head. . . ."

Of course in the course of my life, I learned that they CAN take what's in your head, but I never forgot the first part of my grandmother's admonition: "Never be afraid." Fearlessness (which has sometimes been described as recklessness) has followed me through a long career as a sculptor and writer. I wanted to read about historical truths that had somehow been "taken away" from history: Sally Hemings of Monticello and her daughter Harriet, Nak-shi-dil of Topkapi, Joseph Cinque of the Amistad, Anna Mckinsie of Montreal, my 18th-century fugitive great, great, grandmother, Cleopatra, Not according to Plutarch, and, most recently, Sarah Baartman, the mother of scientific racism, known as the Hottentot Venus.

Each time my grandmother's words come back to me "Never be afraid" and the stubborn five-year-old voice still in my head repeats, "My mother doesn't cover me up." Words that can still get me into a whole lot of trouble. But as the great 20th-century Russian poet Anna Akhmatova put it. "A poet is someone you can never give anything to and you can never take anything away from." Just like my grandmother said.

Christine Choy
Artist, Filmmaker, Teacher

When you meet Christine Choy, you understand her success as a filmmaker as well as her resilience. She had the ability to leave her country and move to another, where she first studied one profession—architecture—and then another—filmmaking—and succeeded in it. Choy is filled with optimism and ideas. When you talk with her, you feel that anything is possible.

Christine Choy is an Oscar-nominated filmmaker and Chair of the Graduate Film and Television Department at New York University. A vanguard filmmaker, who has completed more than 50 films since 1972, she is best known for the Academy Award-nominated *Who Killed Vincent Chin? Ha Ha Shanghai, Homes Apart: The Two Koreas, The Shot Heard 'Round the World.* She received a special tribute at the Hong Kong International Film Festival and screenings at Sundance, Cannes, the International Documentary Festival Amsterdam, Athens International Film Festival, and the San Francisco International Film Festival.

Born in Shanghai, Choy left China for South Korea at the age of nine to join her father who had earlier returned to his home there. "It was 1962 and no one was allowed to leave China. My mother wrote a letter to Chairman Mao entreating that it was important for our family to be reunited. Somehow, we got a visa." When her mother got permission to leave, she gave their house to the government in exchange for the money she needed to travel.

Choy arrived in the United States as a high school student, then trained as an architect at Princeton University, and received a master's degree in urban planning from Columbia University. At Columbia, "students were making films and I thought it was fascinating, but they didn't want to include me.

The majority [of them] were white, male, upper middle class. They were making films about poor people and prisons. I thought it quite peculiar," she recalls.

Choy's filmmaking debut was in the mid-1970s at the Museum of Modern Art in New York. The film was *From Spikes to Spindles*, a documentary about the migration of Chinese immigrants from the West Coast to New York's Chinatown.

She is the recipient of numerous awards, including a Peabody; and fellowships, including a Rockefeller, a Guggenheim, and a Mellon. She is also a founder of Third World Newsreel, a network of radical filmmakers committed to activism and to developing artists and audiences of color.

Christine has an equally impressive history as an educator, teaching not only at New York University at both the undergraduate and graduate levels and chairing the Graduate Division, but also at Yale University, Cornell University, and the State University of New York at Buffalo.

Christine Choy
Imagination and Creativity

Be loyal to your friends and family, be loyal to your art.

There are a lot of kids in the U.S. today who are truly living in two cultures. Maybe they were born in another country and immigrated here, and now have to negotiate two completely different cultures. Maybe these same children have come here with parents who are still rooted in the old country's ways and don't learn English as quickly. Or maybe they're Americans but don't have the advantage of a level

Source: Printed with permission from Christine Choy, Chair, Graduate Film & TV New York University.

playing field, since they are members of a racial minority or an economic class that has to struggle to overcome bigotry or deprivation.

With me, it was all of the above. I grew up in four different countries, with four different political systems, by the time I was 14. I was born in Shanghai, in Communist China, which the U.S. considered a real evil empire back in the 1950s and 1960s. Then we moved to Hong Kong, still under British rule, one of the last colonies of the Empire to gain its autonomy. Then we lived in Seoul, Korea (my father had been in the anti-Japanese resistance movement during World War II), a place that was then under neocolonial military rule. Finally, in the mid-1960s, still a teenager; I learned what it was like to live in an advanced capitalist society here in the United States.

I wish I had the energy to argue with my American teachers back in the 1960s when they started warning us about the evils of Communism, boasting of the prosperity of Hong Kong, justifying the division of Korea, and worshipping the great democracy that is America. Their arguments didn't make any sense to me at all, because I grew up in China. I knew that people didn't have horns on their heads and I knew that our diapers weren't red. Yes, of course, I was indoctrinated in Marxist ideology, just as American kids learn at an early age the value of "shop till you drop."

I grew up in a Shanghai that was vastly different from the thriving city of skyscrapers that it is today. No cars, no traffic, no Toys 'R Us. Our most cherished playthings came from our deepest imagination, with the help of candy wrappers, twigs from trees, and sand. Very elemental things. No frills, no luxuries. But this is how my encounter with the world began. Even today, so many decades later, my films have a direct association with that experience. I was privileged to have a childhood in which imagination and creativity was not stifled by consumerism or materialism.

When I arrived in Hong Kong—quite a cosmopolitan city compared to Shanghai then—my mother's friend, Auntie Doreen, gave me my first Barbie doll. I was fascinated. It looked like a miniature perfect version of Auntie Doreen herself, with a perfect bust and perfect legs. I was puzzled. If this was a British colony, why didn't I get a Queen Elizabeth doll? There I was, thinking outside the box already.

Soon we arrived in Korea, divided in two, occupied by Americans, and ruled under the iron fist of a dictator named Park. It was a noisy place. Outside my window I heard the clash of student demonstrations. Through the walls I listened to the sounds of husbands beating their wives. I had to escape, so on weekends I escaped to the movies and lost myself in Hollywood films. For a few hours, I could forget the discrepancies of society. Thinking outside the box again.

Candy wrappers, Barbie dolls, Hollywood films—these were the ingredients of my early imaginative life. But just like China did under Mao, I took my own Great Leap Forward. I decided that imagination was not enough, that I had to translate this into a meaningful and productive life. I decided to come to the United States to fulfill my American dream. I arrived here with $60 in my pocket and dreams of being a space scientist, if not a nuclear physicist. This was, after all, during the 1960s, when America was pursuing so many dreams— landing on the moon, achieving liberty and justice for all at home while, ironically, trying to impose its military might on Vietnam. It was a frantic and contradictory period, one that could be especially daunting for a scrawny Asian girl now casting her lot in the great land of Barbie dolls, with perfect white bodies.

Even though I'd lived in China, Hong Kong, and Korea, it really sank in for me that I was a foreigner now and that to be accepted as intelligent, artistic, and as a human being, I'd have to formulate a whole new agenda. I had to take a long hard look at who I was perceived to be, who I really was, and who I really wanted to be.

This struggle took place not only intellectually, but psychologically. Ultimately, it forged a great transformation within me. I had to recognize my deficiencies and be totally critical —neither overestimating my weaknesses nor devaluing my strength. Film was my passion. I finally realized that. It helped make me who I am today, an Asian woman, sitting in the chair of the Graduate Film department at the Tisch School of the Arts at New York University.

Yeah, I've come a long way, baby. If I could address my colleagues and students and my future with just a simple phrase, I'd say, "be loyal to your friends and family, be loyal to your art."

John Westermann
Writer

John Westermann's career has been shaped by a life of detours. His father, a lawyer who grew up on Manhattan's Park Avenue and rose to become Chief Executive Officer of the defense contractor Hazeltine Corp., had wanted his son to follow in his footsteps at Columbia University, but John wanted to attend Princeton University. In the end, he went to Trinity College in Hartford, where he did not do well. In fact, he ranked 312 in a class of 314. After his third year, Westermann simply couldn't convince his father that it was worthwhile sending him for a fourth year.

He returned to Long Island, married his high school sweetheart, and moved into uncharted territory. He became a bartender, then a security guard, and finally a village cop. "Besides being a cop, I was the son of a CEO, brother of a lawyer, brother of a doctor—a really privileged childhood," Westermann said. "I sort of failed my way to the police department." He never rose beyond the rank of patrolman, even though he placed first three times in the civil service sergeant's exam. He attributes this to the apparent disapproval of Long Island Republican politicians. "Not getting promoted spurred me to start writing," he said. "I was caught in a civil service trap. . . . I was going to suck it up and stay. Then I began taking notes."

He started with articles for a Freeport weekly, then *The Blotter*, a local police publication. Eventually, he thought about converting his police experiences into fiction. He schooled himself by reading how-to books on writing fiction, and after nine years, 11 rewrites, and countless rejections, sold his first novel, *High Crimes*, to Soho Press in 1988.

John Westermann
Never Quit

Work on your weaknesses. Learn to go left.

While my high school mates got their diplomas, I got a security job during the daylight hours and a bartending job at night, and I grumbled and moaned while I waited to join a police department. I flunked out of college after three years of lacrosse and football, and returned to Long Island a failure.

But now, I'm a retired police officer and the author of five crime novels, one of which, *Exit Wounds*, was made into a hit movie starring Steven Segall and DMX. Sounds cool, but before *Exit Wounds* was a movie, or even a book, it was eleven drafts over eight years, on a manual typewriter. Before that it was a street cop's dream. The security job meant days in a booth at the edge of a huge parking lot, killing eight hours, reading the piles of paperback mysteries under the counter. I knocked off maybe two hundred crime novels that year before I was called to the police academy. Turned out to be a useful senior year, where I was headed. One cop I worked with told me he had never read a whole book. He didn't understand how I would have the audacity to think I could write one.

Five years later, as a cop, I covered a sad and gruesome homicide. I drove home from work and wrote about it, and discovered I liked writing—the fixing and pruning of sentences, sifting for best word, the image that transports, the performance aspect of the process. Dialogue, I love writing dialogue. Plotting, I detest, a defect not faced that cost me years. (Take-home lesson: Work on your weaknesses. Learn

---

Source: Printed with permission from John Westermann.

to go left.) And don't quit, ever. Eight years with no outward signs of success and endless stationhouse criticism preceded the phone call from the agent that led to the book that led to the movie. I might have quit a month too soon and never known how close I came. Talk about an exit wound. Yikes. If you love the work, you are doing what you should be doing. So don't quit. Chin up. You are ahead of the game. Things can only improve with practice.

THE LEADERS

Robert D. Hormats
Economist, Financier, Ambassador

Whether serving the public or private sector, Robert Hormats' expertise in international affairs, business, and finance is unparalleled. He is Vice Chairman of Goldman Sachs (International) and Managing Director of Goldman, Sachs & Co. He joined Goldman Sachs in 1982 after serving as Assistant Secretary of State for Economic and Business Affairs from 1981 to 1982, Ambassador and Deputy U.S. Trade Representative from 1979 to 1981, and as Senior Deputy Assistant Secretary for Economic and Business Affairs at the Department of State from 1977 to 1979.

He served as a senior staff member for International Economic Affairs on the National Security Council from 1969 to 1977, during which time he was senior economic adviser to Dr. Henry Kissinger, General Brent Scowcroft, and Dr. Zbigniew Brzezinski. These global experiences at a relatively young age helped shape the life he was going to live, the mission he was going to pursue, and the professional road he was going to travel. Over the years, he has developed a reputation as one of the world's top investment bankers, and as a man who has a quick grasp on any international issue and is willing to run with it.

44

Robert D. Hormats
Run Your Own Race

In life, the challenge and the thrill is not to succeed at easy things —it is to succeed at *difficult* things.

One lesson I learned early on is that no one is good at everything. If you become unhappy because someone in a room or in your class or in your group of friends is smarter than you, better looking than you, richer than you, or has cooler clothes than you, you are bound to be unhappy all of your life because inevitably someone will be smarter, richer, etc. Each of us has some exceptional talent—some of us are good at one thing and not another, some excel at kindness to others and human empathy, some at sports, some at math, some at selling, and some at managing others. Develop your best talents and do not dwell on what you are not good at. And do not become distracted by people who try to bring you down or make you feel inferior just because you cannot do precisely what they can do. Eleanor Roosevelt put it well, "No one can make you feel inferior without your consent." So don't consent to it.

A good analogy is that of a thoroughbred racehorse, the horse is fitted with blinders so that it cannot see the horses on either side, so that it is not distracted by them and therefore focuses on running its own race. Run your own race.

I grew up in a middle-class neighborhood in Baltimore, first attending a private school through eighth grade, then moving to a public high school that offered advanced courses in language, science, and history. I attended Tufts University, majoring in economics and political science, and then stayed

---

Source: Printed with permission from Robert D. Hormats.

on to do graduate work at the Fletcher School of Law and Diplomacy.

As an undergraduate, I spent one very special summer on a project called Operation Crossroads Africa—a three-month Peace Corps type experience—building fences and barns in rural Kenya. It was my first trip abroad. For a kid from a southern city, it was eye opening to live in a dramatically different society—ethnically and economically. Happily for me, I had previously had at least a limited exposure to kids from other countries—at the age of 10 my parents had sent me to a wonderful summer camp in the Poconos, run by a lovely Quaker family who recruited the children of UN diplomats and councilors from around the world.

Helped by my African experience, I was selected during my first year in graduate school to be a summer intern in the African Affairs Bureau of the State Department. The next year, I was selected to be a summer intern in the U.S. Embassy in Bonn, Germany—where my study of German in high school proved invaluable. It was during the Cold War—and I was intrigued by visits to West and East Berlin, then divided by the Wall.

Toward the end of my last year in graduate school, I was asked to join the economic staff of Dr. Henry Kissinger; he had been recently selected as National Security Advisor to the newly elected President Nixon. An earlier graduate of the Fletcher School, Fred Bergsten, headed the three-person economic staff. Of the three, I was the most junior. Later I moved to the State Department as Deputy Assistant Secretary of State for Economic Affairs, and then became Deputy U.S. Trade Representative and then Assistant Secretary of State for Economic Affairs. In 1982 I left to join Goldman Sachs in New York, where I am now Vice Chairman of Goldman Sachs (International) and a Managing Director.

In looking back over my career, several important moments stand out. One night in college I was struggling with a tough math problem on a take-home exam; my inclination after about an hour of fruitless effort was to conclude that it could not be done—and throw the paper out of the window. Then I decided that of course it could be done—that this problem was in the test precisely to pose a challenge far greater than the other problems. If it were easy everyone could get it. It was there precisely because it was supposed to be difficult. I was determined to do it—and with a change in attitude I succeeded in getting it done and turned out to be one of just two in the class who did. The conclusion I came to was that in life, the challenge and the thrill is not to succeed at *easy* things—it is to succeed at *difficult* things.

Later, in reflecting on my experience working with Dr. Kissinger, I was struck by the same phenomenon—the thrill of working for him was that he demanded far more of his very young staff than we ever thought we could do. And that experience led most of us to accomplish more in that job and then later in life than we ever could have imagined.

Louis Pasteur, the great French scientist, spoke of the "prepared mind." Read, learn, and experience as much as you can. We do not always know which piece of knowledge, bit of information, or experience will be valuable to us tomorrow or next week or next year. When we least expect it, something we have heard or learned or experienced can make all the difference. Success is about building on experiences. Few people achieve instant success—even if it sometimes appears that way. It requires a lot of work and training to be a great musician, doctor, artist, or scientist. Sir Isaac Newton was not the first person to see an apple drop from a tree, yet when he saw it, it opened a whole new science because his mind was prepared by years of experience and study; the insight enabled him to understand the force of gravity. Preparing your mind—in school, through reading, through your life's experience—will enable you to do great things later on.

Recognize that the essence of life is people. Treat others as you would like to be treated. As one very wise person once said to me, "If you can't be anything else, be nice," a simple but lovely concept. One way I often judge the character of others is whether they are as respectful and kind to a waiter or a taxi driver as they are to their boss or someone in authority.

Because life is about people, it is important to make good friends throughout your life, but almost invariably, those friends you make in your earlier years are the best and truest ones—the ones you can rely on not only when things are great but also when things are not so good. Friends can be great in your career, helping you to find a job, helping you to make changes in your life when you are not satisfied with what you are doing, helping you to get back on track if you have a problem.

The time I spent in Africa—where many people live in small villages—showed me a part of our early culture that we sometimes miss. If we go back far enough, we all come from small bands or tribes. Our ancestors all lived in small villages—in Europe, the Middle East, Africa, Asia, and throughout America—wherever we came from. People looked after one another and cared about one another and helped with school-work and farm work. We don't live like that in America any-more, but the basic concepts of reinforcing and reaffirming ties of family and friendship are important.

Finally, one thing stands out from my time in Washington. I saw a president destroyed by lies he himself fashioned with a small coterie of staff. The night President Nixon resigned, a very wise senator reflected over dinner: If you leave Washington with one thing, he said, it should be with a reputation for integrity. If you lose that you have nothing. There are enormous temptations to cut corners, to try to deceive others in order to achieve a certain objective, to succeed at the expense or others or by putting others down, but in the end if you lose your integrity, the chances are others will know and will think less of you for it—and even if they don't know it, *you* will think less of yourself.

For each of you the sky is the limit. Your parents and your teachers can give you wings—but it is up to you to soar on your own—and there is not a single one of you who can't.

Michael R. Bloomberg
Mayor, Entrepreneur

Does a man like Mike Bloomberg need an introduction? Yes and no. We know he is an entrepreneurial billionaire who pioneered a state-of-the art system for reporting and interpreting financial data. We know he is a devoted father and son. But what would make a man who is literally on top of the world take a step to a parallel universe and want to become mayor of New York City?

Michael R. Bloomberg is the 108th Mayor of the City of New York. He was born on February 14, 1942, to middle-class parents in Medford, Massachusetts, where his father was the bookkeeper at a local dairy. After his college graduation, he earned an MBA from Harvard University. In the summer of 1966, he was hired by Salomon Brothers to work on Wall Street.

He founded the Bloomberg LP in 1981, turning an initial order for 20 terminals into a multimedia, analytical news service supplying information to almost every country. Bloomberg Financial Markets is a global distributor of information services, combining news, data, and analysis for global financial markets and businesses. As the business proved its viability, the company branched out and in 1990 Bloomberg LP entered the media business, launching a news service and then radio, television, Internet, and publishing operations. Bloomberg Financial Markets has revolutionized financial communication.

What were the experiences that had such a marked effect on the person Mike Bloomberg is today? Did he apprentice during his childhood years for a business titan (is that how he became this giant of industry and leader of the capital of the world?)? His narrative surprises us and gives us some insight into what strong cultural programming—a summer at boy scout camp and exceptional leadership—can do for a child's sense of self.

Michael R. Bloomberg
Listen, Question, Test, Think

I learned to both be self-sufficient and, simultaneously, to live and work with others.

When I think back on the moments in my life that motivated and inspired me the most, my mind always drifts back to my childhood days in Boston.

Boy Scout summer camp was the highlight of the year. Accommodations were two-man tents under the stars for six weeks in the wilds of New Hampshire. A bugle blew reveille in the morning. We showered under ice-cold water. The food was hot dog and hamburger fare in a big mess hall where everyone took turns peeling potatoes, setting the tables, doing the dishes. I remember loving the meals, particularly the grape-flavored punch called "bug juice." Daily, there were riflery, archery, rowing, canoeing, swimming, art, ceramics, and dozens of other games and skills. Hikes and river trips were the highlight of the week—and parents came to bothersome visiting days only once or twice in the whole summer. It was the time I learned to both be self-sufficient and, simultaneously, to live and work with others.

On Saturday mornings in the winter, I went to the Boston Museum of Science for lectures that introduced the natural and physical world in a way my school could not. Each week, for two hours, I sat spellbound as an instructor brought snakes, porcupines, and owls for us to hold; demonstrated the basic laws of physics with hands-on experiments; and quizzed us on every museum exhibit. All the kids—including me—tried to show off by having every answer. This competition taught the value of precise observation, attention to detail, and careful

---

Source: Michael R. Bloomberg, *Bloomberg by Bloomberg* (New York: Wiley, 2001). Printed with permission.

listening. Once the question concerned the age of a tree whose five-foot cross-section was displayed in the museum upstairs. The exhibit had great historical events marked by a light bulb at each appropriate tree ring, from the current-day outside circle back to the tree's germination centuries earlier, at the center of the display. The question was asked about "the redwood tree." We were suitably frustrated by an instructor who refused to accept what we all knew was the "right" answer, until someone realized the tree cross-section was not from a redwood at all, but rather from a giant sequoia—a related but slightly different variety. Listen, question, test, think: Those instructors taught me the value of intellectual honesty and scholarship years before college.

Richard "Mike" Mullane
Astronaut, Writer

The best expression to be used for Mike Mullane is "the more you do . . . the more you do." NASA selected him in 1978 as a mission specialist in the first group of space shuttle astronauts. He completed three space missions and logged 356 hours in space aboard the *Discovery* (STS-41D), *Atlantis* (STS-27), and *Atlantis* (STS-36).

He was inducted into the International Space Hall of Fame and is the recipient of many awards including the Air Force Distinguished Flying Cross, the Legion of Merit, and the NASA Space Flight Medal.

His devotion to the education of children is well known. He is an award-winning writer of the children's book, *Liftoff! An Astronaut's Dream*. His books and children's videos have been well received. He has also authored, *Do Your Ears Pop in Space?*, a space fact book.

His essay is truly special. It is filled with humility, humor, and determination. His message that "a less than popular" boy can become a man who made his "amazing dream" come true is a real inspiration.

Richard "Mike" Mullane
It Always Counts

I wasn't a gifted star athlete, good looking or popular, yet I had an amazing dream come true.

Whenever I speak to children, I begin with a series of four slides from my high school years. The first slide is my yearbook graduation photo. My ambition reads, "To attend the Air Force Academy." I then tell the children I couldn't get into the Air Force Academy. My grades weren't good enough. I was not a gifted child. I wasn't a genius. But I had the incredible dream of becoming an astronaut come true.

Next, I show a slide from my high school prom. I tell the kids, "I'm not in this photo." I didn't go to either of my high school proms because I couldn't get a date. I wasn't Mr. Good Looking. But I had the incredible dream of becoming an astronaut come true.

The third slide is of the school varsity club. It shows the star athletes in my high school. I tell the kids, "I'm not in this picture." I wasn't a star athlete, yet I had the incredible dream of becoming an astronaut come true.

Finally, I show a fourth slide. This one is of the autograph pages from my high school yearbook. They contain but a single autograph. It reads, "You missed Korea, but here's hoping you make Vietnam." Clearly, I wasn't popular. But I had the incredible dream of becoming an astronaut come true.

I think this sequence of photos is extremely important. It shows how ordinary I was. I wasn't gifted, a star athlete, good looking or popular, yet I had an amazing dream come true.

Source: Printed with permission from Richard "Mike" Mullane, Member, Stories From Space, LLC.

Now, I can see why it happened. I did four things that put me on a path to success. First, I always did my best at whatever I was doing. I didn't worry whether it was going to "count" later in life. Every child should understand this: It *always* counts. Everything you have ever done, everything you will ever do, is going to count in your life, just as it did in mine. Do your best at everything: school, sports, band, scouts, choir, everything!

Second, I always set extremely high goals for myself. Here, I was thinking well outside the box. Early in my life, I set a goal to be a military flyer and ultimately an astronaut. Too many kids set their goals based upon what their parents have done with their lives or what their friends intend to do with theirs or what their brothers and sisters are doing. Forget that! You have your own life. Don't set goals based on others. Set your own goals and set them very high. None of us can be *any*thing we dream to be. We all have boundaries. They might be boundaries of talent A case in point is Michael Jordan. His talent as a basketball player didn't extend to baseball. We might have physical limits: bad eyesight, asthma, diabetes, and so on. My dad was in a wheelchair because of polio. But, within our boundaries, we should be setting the highest possible goals for ourselves. If you shoot for the stars and fall a little short and land on the moon, you haven't failed. You've done yourself a terrific favor. Dream Big!

Third, I never got involved in things that threatened my body, for example, drugs, alcohol abuse, tobacco, or violence. You get one body in life. Whatever dream you are pursuing you're going to need it. Take care of your body!

Finally, I made education my number one priority. I poured heart and soul into my studies. I wasn't gifted, but I got As and Bs through sheer hard work. Kids, know this as a fact. There are laws to protect you from discrimination on the basis of color, religion, gender, etc., but there are no laws to protect you from discrimination on the basis of education. That is a discrimination, which is viscously practiced in this country, and you can't sue anybody if it happens to you. It's legal. You have to protect yourself by getting the best and the most education you possibly can. Make school number one in your life!

It's been my experience the way to get to the stars is to:

Dream Big!
Do your best!
Take care of your body!
Make education number one in your life!

Good luck.

 **Elon Musk**
Entrepreneur

L isted recently in *Fortune* magazine as one of the "40 Richest Under 40," Elon Musk is in the company-launching business. He is widely regarded as one of the most successful Internet entrepreneurs to emerge from the 1990s. Before the age of thirty-two, Elon Musk had founded Zip2, a software company, and sold it to Compaq. He then founded PayPal, the world's leading electronic payment system, which he sold to eBay for $1.5 billion

He is presently personally bankrolling his dream of building rockets with his company SpaceX, a company devoted to reducing the cost and increasing the reliability of access to space.

Born in Pretoria, South Africa, Musk showed entrepreneurial aptitude early. At age twelve, he taught himself to write computer code and designed a game called "Blast Star," a mix of two other popular games. At age seventeen, he moved to Canada. He eventually transferred to the University of Pennsylvania and earned undergraduate degrees in physics and business. He was then off to Silicon Valley to start his company-launching endeavors.

His dreams go further than space exploration, and he has established the Musk Foundation to support philanthropic objectives in education, clean and renewable energy, and medical research.

Elon Musk
Innovation, Drive, and Determination

. . . it is our destiny to go beyond our planet and develop sustainable environments elsewhere.

A s a boy growing up in Pretoria, South Africa, I was fascinated with space and was inspired by the Apollo astronauts. I wanted to one day set foot on the moon or even Mars.

As a huge fan of the popular computer game "Space Invaders," I taught myself how to write computer code and designed my own game called "Blast Star" at the age of 12. I later sold the code to a computer magazine for $500, which back then was a lot of money for a young boy.

It has always been my belief that it is our destiny to go beyond our planet and develop sustainable environments elsewhere. We humans are explorers by nature, that's why we've ventured to the bottom of the oceans and the top of the tallest mountains. That's also why we have sent men to the moon and astronauts to live on the orbiting International Space Station. It was this innate desire for exploration that also motivated me to leave South Africa, at 17, for Canada and then later, the U.S. in pursuit of my dreams.

In the U.S., I decided to enroll at the University of Pennsylvania, where I self-sponsored my education and earned two degrees, in physics and business. I thought the fields of study I chose were essential for any career path I may later take: physics is the basis of all present and future technology, while business skills can turn a technology into a profitable venture.

I must also note that another great source of inspiration for me, which initially sparked my interest in physics, was the

---

Source: Printed with permission from Elon Musk.

futuristic novels written by Jules Verne. I must have read them all so many times that I practically knew them by heart. I was completely mesmerized by how Verne presented glimpses into the future, and envisioned things, such as submarines, space ships, and space voyages, ahead of their times.

After graduation, I was really keen on doing something that could further my understanding of cutting-edge technology. Back then, I paid close attention to the Internet revolution going on in the Silicon Valley and finally said to myself, "I could either watch it happen or be a part of it." That's when I came up with Zip2, a Web software company catering to the media industry, which I started at 23 in the small boarding house where I lived. Times were rough in the beginning, but I believed in my idea and persevered. Only a few years later, I sold Zip2 to Compaq for $307 million. I was fortunate enough in that the success of my first company was followed by another—PayPal, now the largest online payment service. I sold PayPal to eBay in 2001, for $1.5 billion.

Following PayPal, I felt that the moment had come for me to pursue my true vocation and passion for space. After a closer look into the private and government space industries, I was disappointed with the lack of innovation in the field of space exploration since man first landed on the moon almost 34 years ago. I figured that if I wanted to go to space and help us in the quest for other planets, I was better off building my own rocket. In the summer of 2002, I founded Space Exploration Technologies (SpaceX) and employed a great team of about 20 top engineers who shared my vision for space. It must be noted that starting and growing a business is as much about the innovation, drive, and determination of the people behind it as the product they sell. By developing rockets that can launch small to large payloads into space, SpaceX is taking progressive steps toward achieving our goal of successfully flying humans beyond Earth's orbit. And yes, it will all be done in our lifetime.

As I work vigilantly on pursuing my dream of space exploration, I wish to encourage all those who once dreamt of being astronauts to look no further, because it is all within our reach.

Eric Anderson
Entrepreneur

When I asked Mr. Anderson what inspired him to become an *astropreneur* (a term coined by *Wired* magazine), he spoke about the impact the books *2001: A Space Odyssey* by Arthur C. Clarke and *Cosmos* by Carl Sagan, along with the movie *Star Wars*, had on him.

Born in 1974 in Denver, Colorado, Eric Anderson, a leading astropreneur, is the president and Chief Executive Officer of Space Adventures, Ltd. He is an outspoken advocate of commercial space transportation, private space exploration, and space tourism. He cofounded Space Adventures in 1997 with several former astronauts and leading visionaries from the aerospace, adventure travel, and entertainment industries.

Anderson's dream is to open the space frontier to everyone. It is his hope that through the development of the suborbital space flight program he helped engineer and the latest mission to take private explorers to the International Space Station, the company can benefit not only private individuals interested in space travel, but also the international space program as a whole. He shares the belief that space exploration is vital to human progress and believes that by opening the space frontier to private men and women from around the world, we can greatly enhance technological development and cultural understanding.

Previously, Anderson, a former NASA researcher, was the Executive Vice President and cofounder of Starport.com, an astronaut-endorsed space education and entertainment Web site, which was sold to SPACE.com in June 2000.

Eric Anderson
Don't Be Afraid to Take a Chance

If I wasn't going to go to space as an astronaut, I was going to pave my own way to the skies.

E ver since I was a little boy, I have dreamed of building space ships and becoming an astronaut. Inspired by the great explorers of the early days of NASA, who landed on the moon, and by watching fantastic science fiction movies like the *Star Wars* trilogy, I imagined that one day I too could explore the universe. My fascination with space grew throughout my school years because I realized how important it was for the future of humanity to continue exploring space. My favorite class was astronomy, and in elementary school I even built a huge model of the solar system out of wood with little colored planets, which is still on proud display at my parents' house. I also read many great books about space exploration by such authors as Robert Heinlein and Isaac Asimov. My first space book, *Cosmos*, by Carl Sagan, I read in third grade—it was a little difficult but I read every page and enjoyed it very much!

While in high school, I visited the Kennedy Space Center with my family and up to that point, it was one of my life's greatest adventures. Later, I visited the National Air and Space Museum in Washington, DC—another great adventure. I appreciated very much that both my parents were supportive of my passion and interest in space and encouraged that I pursue a degree in space technology. I got accepted at the University of Virginia, where I began study in Aerospace Engineering. I also founded the Space Advancement Society,

Source: Printed with permission by Eric Anderson, President & CEO of Space Adventures.

which is the Virginia chapter for the Students for Exploration and Development and Space (SEDS) and which allowed me to meet many new friends also interested in space exploration.

Also while at the University of Virginia, I had some excellent summer jobs. In my first, I worked at the National Radio Astronomy Observatory studying deep-space galaxies with famous astronomers. I got to travel to the largest telescope in the world, the VLA in Socorro, New Mexico. The next summer, I was selected as the top student from Virginia to enter the NASA Academy program. I learned a lot of leadership skills, met some incredible people, and helped with space shuttle experiments at the NASA Goddard Space Flight Summer. In my last summer job, I worked for a foundation that was offering a prize for the first space tourism vehicles to be built—it was called the X Prize! I continued to maintain close contact and friendships with the people I met in those summer jobs for the rest of my life.

After graduation, I decided not to apply to the NASA astronaut corps because I had imperfect vision, a major impediment to an aspiring astronaut. Although my long-time dream of becoming a professional astronaut would not come to be, I knew I had to seek alternatives to make a positive out of my dream. In 1997, fresh out of college and filled with enthusiasm, I decided to start a space tourism company with the help of travel and aerospace experts such as Buzz Aldrin and other astronauts. If I wasn't going to go to space as an astronaut, I was going to pave my own way to the skies.

What I have now come to realize is that flying in space with NASA is only one way to get into space, and it may even be less exciting than being a private space explorer and pioneer. In the commercial space industry, the possibilities are endless, and they don't depend on having perfect vision or the ups and downs of government budgets. The mission of Space Adventures, the company I am heading, is to open the space frontier to regular people like you and me. We have already had two clients fly to space, and both said it was the most rewarding, inspiring, wonderful life-changing experience they had ever had.

Today's young generation will be able to travel to Earth's orbit, the moon, and beyond, because people continue to have the vision and the courage to innovate. Never give up on your dreams; there are always ways to achieve them. Just be creative and don't be afraid to take a chance in life!

Neil deGrasse Tyson
Astrophysicist

There is no better role model for children who are interested in exploring the universe than Neil deGrasse Tyson, the first Frederick P. Rose Director of the Hayden Planetarium. One of the most respected astrophysicists in the country, he was born and raised in New York City, where he was educated in the public schools from elementary school to his graduation from the Bronx High School of Science. He went on to earn his BA in Physics from Harvard University and his PhD in Astrophysics from Columbia University.

Tyson's professional research interests include star formation, exploding stars, dwarf galaxies, and the structure of the Milky Way. In 2001, Tyson was appointed by President George W. Bush to serve on a 12-member commission that studied the future of the U.S. Aerospace Industry, and in 2004, he was once again appointed by President Bush to serve on a nine-member commission on the Implementation of the U.S. Exploration Policy, dubbed the "Moon, Mars, and Beyond" commission.

In addition to dozens of professional publications, Dr. Tyson has written, and continues to write, for the public. Since January 1995, he has contributed a monthly column, "Universe" to *Natural History* magazine.

Mr. Tyson's personal story is poignant and enlightening. A somewhat "nerdy" black child (not always an easy combination), with a love of astrophysics and the support of his family, he persevered to a position of leadership and innovation. His contributions to the public appreciation of the cosmos have been recognized by the International Astronomical Union with the naming of asteroid "13123 Tyson." On the lighter side, the nerdy kid in 2000 was voted "sexiest astrophysicist alive" by the readers of *People* magazine.

Neil deGrasse Tyson
Reach for Your Own Star

I share the segments of my life's paths that got me here, which, for the most part, were upstream and against the winds of society.

As an astrophysicist and as the Director of New York City's celebrated Hayden Planetarium, I get to decode the nature of the universe and create journeys through it for all the public to see.

What was not apparent, however, was the somewhat peculiar profile that I carried into the job. Although everyone's life is unique, certain categories of life experience can be generalized. My tenure as a nerdy kid—complete with winnings in the science fair, membership in the physics club, and high scores in mathematics—greatly resembles all that you may have stereotyped for the world's community of nerds. My time as an athlete—as captain of my high school's wrestling team and as a varsity competitor in college—was no different from that of any other athlete. My interest in the universe—carrying me to a PhD in astrophysics—led me down paths shared by many of my colleagues. And my life as a black male in America—getting stopped for no reason by the police or being trailed by security guards in department stores—is hardly different from that of other black males among my contemporaries. But when you combine all ingredients, my experiences offer a possibly unique portal through which to view life, society, and the universe.

I want every generation of stargazers—whether they sit atop a tenement roof or an Appalachian Mountain—to have a

---

Source: © Neil deGrasse Tyson 2004. Adapted from *The Sky Is Not the Limit: Adventures of an Urban Astrophysicist* (New York: Prometheus Books, 2004).

fresh lens with which to see the universe and to reach for their own star.

I was just nine years old and had just seen a space show at the Hayden Planetarium, but I now had an answer for that perennially annoying question all adults ask, "What do you want to be when you grow up?" Although I could barely pronounce the word, I would tell them, "I want to be an astrophysicist."

That was the night. The universe poured down from the sky and flowed into my body. I had been called. The study of the universe would be my career, and no force on earth would stop me.

A precocious childhood friend of mine, who lived in my neighborhood, taught me to play chess, poker, pinochle, Risk, and Monopoly. He introduced me to brainteaser books. I loved teasers that involved math. The more we played, the more stretched and sharpened my eleven-year old brain became.

My friend's most important contribution to my life's path, however, was when he introduced me to binoculars and encouraged me to look up. He encouraged me to look beyond the streetlights, beyond the buildings, beyond the clouds, and out toward the moon and stars of the night sky. The moon was no longer just a thing on the sky—it was another world in the universe. I later learned that Galileo's "observatory" was his windowsill and his rooftop. So was mine, having grown up on the eighth floor of the Skyview Apartments in the Bronx.

My sixth grade science teacher, aware of my growing interest in the universe from my book reports, clipped a small advertisement from the newspaper announcing that year's offering of astronomy courses at the Hayden Planetarium. She probably also figured that if my excess social energy were intelligently diverted outside of the school that I could grow in ways unfettered by the formal limits of the classroom. A student's academic life experience can be constructed from much more than what happens in a classroom. Good teachers know this. The best teachers make sure it happens.

From then onward, the Hayden Planetarium became a much broader and deeper resource to the growth of my life's interests. I had previously only known it to be a place with a beautiful night sky—but the actual universe is much, much bigger.

For my thirteenth birthday, I received my first telescope. And I had a backyard where I could observe the heavens for hours and hours without distractions of any kind since my family temporarily moved for one year from the Bronx to Lexington, Massachusetts.

When I was a student in elementary school and junior high school in New York City, I eagerly attended monthly public lectures given by visiting experts on various topics on the universe at the Hayden Planetarium. The speakers were so smart and knew so much that I wanted to be just like them when I grew up. Fifteen years later, I returned to the Planetarium to deliver an invited public lecture of the same monthly series that I had attended as a student. Immediately following my lecture, as if I had passed through a loop in the space-time continuum, a 12-year-old student walked up to me after my lecture and asked, "What should I do to be just like you?" At that moment, I knew that I had helped to plant a dream in someone else the way others before had planted a dream in me.

Word of my cosmic interests spread among my extended relatives and family friends. The family network helped in many and varied ways to provide an intellectual buoyancy to my pursuits. One of my mother's cousins worked in the Brooklyn Public Library and never failed to acquire and send deaccessioned astronomy and math books my way. A close friend of my parents had some expertise in photography and back-and-white film processing. She served as a first mentor in my early days of astrophotography. Another close friend of the family, who happened to be professor of education at The City College of New York, recommended me to one of her colleagues, an instructor at CCNY's Workshop Center for Open Education—a program that offered continued education programs for adults. The instructor, in turn, invited me to give a talk to her fall classes on the cosmos. For me, talking about the universe was like breathing. I suppose it was no different from another kid talking about his treasured baseball card collection or a film buff recalling scenes from a favorite movie. I could not have been more comfortable sharing what I knew.

At age 14, by summer's end, my fate was set: I was a card-carrying member of New York's Amateur Astronomer's Association.

In the fall of my senior year of high school, I applied to five universities, including Harvard, MIT, and Cornell, which were my top three choices. When it came to actually choosing a college to attend, I devised a decision matrix that tallied the number of physics and astronomy articles in *Scientific American* written by scientists who had been undergraduates at the schools that admitted me. I also tallied where these same authors earned their Masters degrees, their PhDs, and where they were currently on the faculty. Harvard won in every category.

My parents never told me where to go or what to learn. In retrospect, that was for the better—because they could not. This ensured that the expression of my life's interests were as pure as space itself. To this day, my parents remain two of the warmest and most caring parents I have known. Of all the places I have been, the troubles I have seen, and the trials I have endured, let there be no doubt that I continually felt their guidance ahead of me, their support behind me, their love beside me.

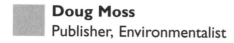

Doug Moss
Publisher, Environmentalist

Doug Moss is a man devoted to the environment. Doug Moss is a businessman. It takes these two qualities to make an environmental publication a success. Doug Moss is the founder, publisher, and executive editor of *E/The Environmental Magazine*, a fifteen-year-old national bimonthly environmental magazine, published in Norwalk, Connecticut, by the not-for-profit Earth Action Network, Inc., which he also founded.

Earth Action Network also publishes books, operates the environmental Web site emagazine.com, and publishes and distributes *EarthTalk*, a weekly question-and-answer column on environmental issues which runs on MSNBC.com, other Web sites, and in 250 U.S. and Canadian newspapers. Doug previously cofounded *The Animals' Agenda*, a bimonthly animal protection magazine, serving as an editor and its first publisher from 1979 until 1988.

He is clearly dedicated to the preservation of our environment, which he has made his life's work, but the businessman in him knows that to pursue this passion, he must keep his eye on the ball—and the bottom line.

Doug Moss
Ambition and Perseverance

I've always "aimed high" in the goals I've set for myself, and I don't give up easily.

If I had to pick two words that sum up why I was able to achieve in life they would be ambition and perseverance. I've always "aimed high" in the goals I've set for myself, and I don't give up easily. In the process, I improve my skills at whatever I'm attempting to do.

My childhood baseball hero, Mickey Mantle, was probably my biggest inspiration, as were the Beatles. Mantle had a bone disease and a history of injuries in one of his legs such that he had to completely wrap his knee in tape before every game. Nonetheless, despite this handicap, he went on to become one of baseball's all-time greatest players and the idol of many because he was also a very modest and likable person. And the Beatles changed popular music forever by not being afraid to be different and by continually working to improve themselves and to try new things along the way.

Because of Mickey Mantle's inspiration, I took up baseball myself and even learned to switch-hit as he did. Because of the Beatles, I taught myself guitar and piano, and I have since written about 25 original melodies myself. My mother also deserves credit. A musician and hard worker herself, she encouraged me to be active and entrepreneurial at the things I enjoyed. As a youngster I had a paper route and also mowed my neighbors' lawns to earn money, while playing throughout my younger years in Little League and Babe Ruth League, and also playing cello in the orchestra.

Source: Printed with permission from Doug Moss, Norwalk, Connecticut.

During the 15 years that I've been publishing *E/The Environmental Magazine*, which is nonprofit and relies on foundation grants for support, I have been the key person responsible for raising money. It's been an uphill battle, and I ,joke with my coworkers at times that I could "wallpaper the whole office" with just the stacks of rejection letters I have in my files. But that has never deterred me. It sounds funny, but sometimes when a "No" arrives in the mail from a foundation from whom I've asked for a grant, it just energizes me to figure out how to get a "Yes" from them next time. I'm quite passionate about the environment and also about the need for our media to serve us properly.

Foundations have not traditionally supported media, preferring instead to fund projects that have clear and measurable short-term consequences, like giving money to build a nature center, where they can see the results of the money they spent standing there right in front of them. But many of the environmental issues we fight for, and the efforts needed to win those fights, are less tangible than that, though still very important—and a magazine like *E* can do a lot to educate people, both young and old, about the importance of safeguarding the environment. I think after years of persevering with the foundations that provide the funding—while at the same time putting out a well-written magazine that is a team effort—I've successfully persuaded them to agree.

I grew up in Norwalk, Connecticut, catching frogs and fishing in local ponds, but I would trace my environmentalism to an event that occurred much later. One day, while living in New Haven, Connecticut, after graduating with a degree in marketing from Babson College in 1974, I watched a TV report about the clubbing of baby harp seals in Newfoundland, Canada (that seal hunt has now resumed in a big way in 2004). I was outraged at what I saw, and my first impulse was to run to the phone to call the TV station to complain that they were televising this. I didn't make the call, realizing that the TV station was only the messenger, not the one killing seals. Coincidentally, a few days later I saw some people in downtown New Haven demonstrating against wearing fur, so I joined the local antifur group. I began to get more and more involved and, in the process, I met a whole community of people who shared my concerns about animals and the environment. I started to spend my free time on such activities as gathering signatures on petitions, organizing events, and working on newsletters.

In 1979, I left the Burroughs Corporation, with which I got a job after college, and started my own company, Douglas Forms. I wanted to "be my own boss" and decided to "take the plunge" now that I knew the business forms field well. In 2004 Douglas Forms celebrated its 25th anniversary. As it turned out, most of my customers were magazine publishers, and I learned a lot from them about the business of magazine publishing. Soon a few of my friends and I decided to publish an animal rights magazine. In late 1979 the first issue of *The Animals' Agenda* appeared.

After nine years of publishing *The Animals' Agenda*, I decided that, while I still supported animal rights concerns, my interests were broadening to include other related concerns. Global warming, medical waste, ozone depletion and other issues gave me and my wife, Deborah, the idea to try our hand at a new nonprofit magazine. I left *The Animals' Agenda* and launched a new, independent magazine that would focus on a broad range of environmental issues.

Work began on *E/The Environmental Magazine* during the "Greenhouse Summer" of 1988, amid reports of medical waste washing up on New Jersey shores, fires in Yellowstone Park, and growing public interest in the environment. *E* debuted—after 18 months of planning, research, and networking with the environmental community—in January 1990, in the wake of the Exxon Valdez disaster and on the eve of the twentieth anniversary of Earth Day, just as people were dubbing the 1990s, "the environmental decade."

All of this has taught me that it's important to "leave no stone unturned" in considering the unlimited opportunities to make the most of even just one project, such as a magazine whose reach can be multiplied exponentially through creative thinking.

Jack J. Cambria
New York Police Department Hostage Negotiator

In New York City, it's not uncommon to turn on the news and see an interview with Lt. Jack Cambria, the Commanding Officer of the NYPD's Hostage Negotiation Team. His demeanor is reserved and modest, even though his job is demanding, high performance, high stress, and critical to saving lives. His job is so compelling and riveting that CBS revolved their program "48 Hours" around him and his competent team.

Cambria is a 22-year veteran of the New York Police Department. Today he coordinates the efforts of one hundred negotiators, who respond to all hostage and related situations throughout the city. He is responsible for the training and certification of new negotiators and the retraining of current negotiators. He conducts in-service training for newly promoted captains, lieutenants, sergeants, and many outside law enforcement agencies. He was temporarily reassigned back to the Emergency Service Unit, where he had served for 16 years, for the three months following the attack on the World Trade Center to assist in the rescue and recovery efforts at Ground Zero.

He earned his Bachelor and Associate of Science degrees in Criminal Justice from the State University of New York, Empire State College and is currently working toward a Masters Degree in Criminal Justice from the John Jay College of Criminal Justice, City University of New York.

Jack J. Cambria
Never Give Up

If you are thrown seven times, you must get up eight.

As I was growing up, the thought of becoming a New York City police officer never crossed my mind. In my teen years I worked at many odd jobs, starting in Brooklyn's Prospect Park ice-skating rink and carousel. I ended up a truck driver for a plumbing supply company, also in Brooklyn. I remember taking a small amount of pride in that position, since I had to work hard to earn the class-3 driver's license required to drive the truck. But as time went on, the work became less and less interesting and my employment status was at the mercy of the store staying in business. I decided to look for something more secure and took several civil service exams, including tests for police officer, firefighter, sanitation worker, and other jobs. When I received the letter from the police department indicating that I had passed its entrance exam, I realized that it was the first time I had a potential career to be zealous about.

In my 21 years with the police department, I have held a host of assignments, each one more challenging than the former. My work has ranged from, as a young policeman, performing precinct foot and radio car patrol to plainclothes anticrime assignments. I spent 16 exciting years with the Emergency Service Unit (ESU), which is a tactical and rescue unit of the NYPD. It was during my time in ESU that I would find myself perched atop various New York City landmarks, such as the Empire State Building, Statue of Liberty, Brooklyn Bridge, in attempts to rescue suicidal individuals and helping end their unremitting emotional pain. I served as a police officer, sergeant, and lieutenant within various precincts

Source: Printed with permission from Jack J. Cambria.

and in ESU and always approached my work with compassion and enthusiasm. The road to realizing my own personal pinnacle of success did not come easily, but rather, was achieved through hard work and perseverance. Reaching the rank of lieutenant was only realized after taking two sergeant and two lieutenant exams, which are given approximately five years apart. I think if I had been discouraged after failing my first sergeant's test, I would never have had the job I now hold and my life would have been drastically different.

My current, and probably my last, assignment in the police department, is as commanding officer of the Hostage Negotiation Team. Hostage negotiators are detectives who are asked to attempt to resolve high-crisis situations using only their words, thereby preventing a tactical deployment of the police into a hostile environment. It is always better and safer to have dangerous individuals come out to us, than to go in after them. Complicated and interpersonal maneuverings are employed in attempting to resolve these types of situations.

Perhaps the most arduous test of my fortitude came on September 11, 2001. I first arrived at the World Trade Center some 30 minutes after the South Tower had fallen, and I remained there until late November, spending an average of 16 hours a day at the site to assist in the rescue and then recovery effort. My experiences while assigned at Ground Zero will be forever etched in my mind. Fourteen of the victims were police officers assigned to ESU, whom I had the privilege of personally serving with over the years. I also lost some very close personal friends that day.

Several years ago, I was involved in martial arts training, and I learned a very simple philosophy, which is so easily applied to life: *If you are thrown seven times, you must get up eight.* I think if we let ourselves be discouraged by life's various obstacles, we would not follow our dreams in pursuit of our personal successes.

Mark Norell
Paleontologist

Mark Norell's work has taken him around the globe, ever since he began going on scientific expeditions at the age of 14. His life's work—exploring for dinosaurs—has taken him on 20 international expeditions. In the last few years, he has worked actively in Patagonia, Cuba, the Chilean Andes, the Sahara, West Africa, and Mongolia. In 1989, Dr. Norell accepted a curatorial position at the American Museum of Natural History in New York, and he is now chairman and curator of its Division of Paleontology.

According to the museum's Web site, Norell's accomplishments include the discovery of the richest Cretaceous fossil locality in the world, the first embryo of a theropod dinosaur, and the first indication of a dinosaur nesting on a clutch of eggs like a bird.

His work regularly appears in major scientific journals (including cover stories in *Science* and *Nature*), and he was cited by *Time* magazine for one of the 10 most significant science stories of 1994 and 1996, and in 1993, 1994, and 1996 as the author of one of *Discover* magazine's top 50 science stories of the year.

Between expeditions and the demands of a scientific career, Dr. Norell lectures to the general public and writes books and articles for diverse audiences. The second edition of *Discovering Dinosaurs* won *Scientific American*'s Young Readers Book of the Year Award.

Mark Norell
Work Hard, Play Hard, Think Hard, Finish Stuff

People should learn as much about as many different things as possible. . . .

I have always been very fortunate. I was raised in suburban Los Angeles when dairy farms and orange groves were a short bike ride away—and the beach was close enough that the sand and waves were frequently visited. Such an environment was conducive to a kid interested in science and at home outdoors. There were fossils to be found, insects to be captured, and birds and gophers to be massacred. I had tolerant and supportive parents. So tolerant that I convinced them to carry large plastic garbage bags in the car trunk on family outings so I could harvest interesting road kill for my anatomical collection.

School was of interest to me and because of this it always seemed easy. I had some excellent if not memorable teachers. My greatest education, however, came through the science programs at the Los Angeles County Museum of Natural History. There, I was exposed to real scientists working on projects around the globe. I was able to volunteer in different departments and accompany field trips to the California deserts and Mexico to collect mammals and reptiles, survey whale populations and, most of all, collect fossils. This was different from the science that I was taught in school. This sort of science was creative and fun. Since this was the early 1970s, the scientists I got to know were not stereotypical nerd-scientists, but an inspired, fun-loving tribe.

In college my mind was made up. I wanted to pursue science as a career. I continued to accompany fossil collecting

---

Source: Printed with permission from Mark Norell.

expeditions to the American West. Following my undergraduate education I pursued my masters at San Diego, where I
came in contact with an exceptional group of young scientists and learned how to do research. From there I went to
Yale University to work on my PhD. Even though my interests
wavered (at one point I was studying the molecular genetics
of transposons in maize), when I finished my PhD I realized
that I was really good at science.

I left with the feeling that I could work on almost anything. No matter what it was, it was just another data set that
needed to be looked at rationally and empirically. When I was
offered my job at the American Museum of Natural History, I
had never worked on dinosaurs. They simply put the question
to me "If we hire you will you work on dinosaurs?" Throughout all this I stayed focused on what made me interested in
science as a child, always wondering why and how you can
use theory and evidence (data) to understand some basic
things about how the world works.

Even though I work on the past, it is very important to
think in the present and beyond. Curiosity and imagination
are crucial, and you should instinctively look for the next
best thing, the thing that is just beyond the horizon. But this
is not enough. A common saying in my field is that ideas are
cheap—even good ones. It is their implementation and development that is difficult. There is no substitute for hard work,
and there is no excuse for not finishing projects and other
things in a timely fashion. If I look around, I have known
some amazing thinkers. Those who were finishers went on to
become luminaries. That does not make them necessarily any
smarter than many of the rest. It has, however, made them
more successful.

All of us will have setbacks during our careers and lives.
Personal tragedy, illness, and the like—these are not pleasant
things. Looking back, there are things that I would change

and much that I wished that I never experienced. Nevertheless, the spectrum of experience is good and makes an archive that is my most important tool in going forward with my work and life.

The idea of a wide spectrum also forms the core about my philosophy of education. People should learn as much about as many different things as possible—and not just academic subjects. You would be surprised how knowing how to fix a car, install drywall, or cook a soufflé aids a scientist. And for inspiration? Each person is inspired in a different way. My own comes just from living and realizing that I have an obligation to my family and others. Ideas come at weird times—recently I've gotten a lot of thinking done just walking around listening to Metallica and old punk rock—Sex Pistols, X, and the like.

My advice: work hard, play hard, think hard, finish stuff, surround yourself with the same kind of people, listen to them, be an information magnet, experience all you can. Combined with a little luck, this will take you a long way.

John A. Hays
Deputy Chairman, Christie's, North and South America

H aving been with Christie's auction house for more than 20 years, John Hays is involved in developing business strategies for the sale of top American art collections. Hays joined Christie's in 1983, and ever since has played an instrumental role in bringing innovation and record-setting sales to the field of American furniture and folk art. In addition to being Deputy Chairman, he is Principal Auctioneer and oversees the age-old practice of buying and selling things of value and interest for collectors. Mr. Hays has orchestrated and presided over a record-breaking series of Americana sales.

How does an all-American boy end up selling to the eclectic and elite collectors of the world? He set his mind to it.

John A. Hays
You Can Do Anything If You Set Your Mind to It

If you know you can get out from the bottom—you won't be afraid to try your moves on the top.

I was lucky. I came from a family that believed their children could do anything they wanted—no matter how unrealistic the idea or far-fetched it sounded. In some ways this made it difficult, as we really believed we could do anything and for a brief moment I thought I would like to be a sculptor. But looking back on the experience, I remember how seriously everyone took me and the awful clay mounds that I created. Still, my effort did make me realize that confidence was everything. If people believed in you, you believed in yourself.

Source: Printed with permission from John A. Hays.

I went to Phillips Exeter Academy and made the varsity wrestling team in the 10th grade. The coach, Ted Seabrooke, was a former "Big Ten" wrestling champ from Oklahoma A&M. He had a gift for making skinny 130 pound kids feel like they could beat anybody in this sport—and we did. He used to say "If you KNOW you can get out from the bottom—you won't be afraid to try your moves on the top." And so we worked hard at that strategy and ended up winning matches against kids far stronger than we were but who didn't have the confidence we had! I remember being in the finals of a tournament where I was behind 10 to 1. The other guy got a little careless and I got free and pinned him with only a few seconds left. Never give up!

I went to Kenyon College (a bit "outside the box" since my family traditionally went to Harvard University). I fell in love with the Art Department and one thing led to another. I actually got a job in the art world when I graduated. Today, at Christie's, I am a principal auctioneer for the firm, but I think of those days wrestling at Exeter whenever I step into the podium to take a sale: confident that I can run a sale no matter who I'm in front of, believing that you can do anything if you set your mind to it.

Joseph Denofrio
Senior Vice President for Fashion, Macy's

Joseph Denofrio, a New Jersey native, completed 16 years of education in the Catholic school system. Graduating from Seton Hall University with a BA in government, he immediately began a retail career with Macy's through its college recruitment program.

Although home has never exceeded a 10 mile radius, business travel for product development has provided exposure to various cultures, life styles, and standards of living around the world.

Looking back on his school years, Joe credits the Boy Scouts National Honor Society and serving as business manager of his high school's yearbook as key experiences that prepared him for the business world. Eventually, he became Senior Vice President of Fashion for Macy's and spent much time developing his expertise in women's and men's fashion, to complement his retail experience in home furnishings.

Joseph Denofrio
Aim High

I guess aiming high works as well in the candy business as it does in the courtroom.

Time goes by quickly when we're having fun and doing something we like. That is the one thing that we all have in common, and that's how I feel about the years that I have spent working in the retail business. It's been a lot of hard work, mind you, but always fun. No matter what else I've

Source: Printed with permission from Joseph Denofrio.

tried, no matter where others attempted to lead me, the one consistent source of fun for me was, and still is, the search for that perfect item on my shopping list.

These items have changed over the years. The earliest search that I can remember was for a box of 64 Crayola Crayons with the built-in pencil sharpener. I found it and have been shopping ever since. My most recent search has been for a log cabin built on a lake. I am happy to say that as of this writing, I am sitting in the kitchen of my dream home, overlooking that lake.

In between the crayons and the lake is more than 35 years in the retail business that has brought me from my first job in the world's smallest candy store to Macy's—"the world's largest department store." When I was 12, the owner of my local candy store asked me if I wanted to work for him during my summer vacation. I started working four hours a day for a dollar an hour and still remember receiving my first $20 bill in a bank envelope. Looking at pictures of myself during this time in my life, I think I must have spent my entire pay right there in the candy store!

Carl, the owner of the store, was the first of several role models who over the years taught me about personal proprietorship. Carl's name was on that store, and he worked hard to ensure that it was the best that it could possibly be. I remember, even at 12, feeling very proud that he had entrusted me with certain duties that he said no one did better than I. Today, I delegated a task to someone at work and told him it was because he could perform it better than I could. He did. Thanks Carl.

This job continued through my high school years. I did great at school. I scored very high on the standardized tests and received a lot of advice to aim for a conventional profession. The guidance counselors kept repeating "law school," but my mind was on planning the best candy and ice cream presentations anywhere. I guess aiming high works as well in the candy business as it does in the courtroom.

College was very important. I attended a university that had its own law school and I did well during my four years there. I was accepted to continue on, and join the law program. The two most important realizations that I had during my college years were:

1. That there were a lot of talented and capable people sitting next to me in class and working hard would be the only way that I could measure up.
2. I couldn't wait until 4:00 PM every weekday. That was the time that I went to my job at the local department store.

Putting realizations 1 and 2 together, I accepted a job in Macy's Executive Training Program, after a college recruiter came to visit my campus.

Twenty-five years later, I was still working hard at what I loved. I felt as energized before retirement as I did the day I started. I have now covered every level of management from executive trainee through senior vice president. Some jobs during the years were harder than others. I stuck with it because the retail operation never stopped exciting me. As I climbed through management, I never forgot how proud my first boss Carl was to have his name on the front of his store. I guess you can call me "Joe Macy." I'll always appreciate that someone recognized dedication and talent in me. I'd like to return that favor to all of you talented future retailers.

Always remember:

> Put your name on it,
> Find your role models,

Discover what it is that no one else can do better than you,
Keep your eyes open for the talents in others,

And most important,

Have fun and you'll have a happy and successful career.

John R. Passarini
Educator, Coach

John R. Passarini is a phenomenal educator because to him it all begins with caring and heart. The second you engage him in conversation, he teaches by example that if you respect people for who they are, it enhances their self-esteem. That's who John Passarini is! John R. Passarini has been a teacher for 34 years. He holds an EdD in Special Education. He taught physical education and health in the Waltham Public Schools for 18 years, and founded the Waltham High School wrestling team, which he coached for 13 years. For the past 16 years John has taught adapted physical education in the Wayland Public Schools. He is in the process of retiring from teaching with the goal of becoming an educational consultant.

In 2002, John was named the Adapted Physical Education National Teacher of the Year by the American Association for Active Lifestyles and Fitness and in 2003, he received the prestigious honor of being named the Disney Outstanding Teacher of the Year. A parent of one of John's students said, "To me, Coach Pass personifies the truth that each child is worth it, and it was his incredible faith in Katie that set her spirit free."

He is a national teaching treasure. He teaches out of the box.

John R. Passarini
Limited Only by Our Thoughts

If you set goals, love what you do, stay focused, and pursue your dreams with passion and perseverance, your teachers will appear.

I grew up in a bilingual home with lots of love, lots of support, and good food, but few books. My mother, Dorina, was born in Italy and only got through the third grade. My father, Adolpho, was born with cerebral palsy and contracted polio at age 6. He did not walk until he was 14 years old and because of his physical and learning challenges, he did not graduate from high school until he was 20. He never complained.

My parents taught me how to be a good person and how to love life, but my language and reading skills lagged behind. When I was forced to repeat second grade in 1955, I was disappointed and confused. Nobody ever explained why this happened and for several years I was sad and self-conscious.

In May 2001, I received my doctorate in education from Boston University. In 2003, I was named Disney's Outstanding Teacher of the Year. What happened? My strong athletic and social skills carried me through elementary school. I was embarrassed by my poor academic skills, but I had good self-esteem, lots of friends, and a positive attitude. Most important, I had clear goals and a strong desire to succeed.

My academic struggles continued in junior high school until I met Warren E. Priest. Warren was an English and social studies teacher who recognized my potential and appreciated my desire to improve my academic skills. When I met Warren I was "ready" to learn. Warren had me read aloud. He

---

Source: Printed with permission from John R. Passarini, Teacher, Leader.

gave me extra spelling tests. He gave me extra writing assignments, which he generously marked up with his dreaded red pen. Eventually, the sea of red dwindled to a few scattered blotches. Now, although spelling remains a challenge, I love to write.

At Newton South High School, my reading skills were still not perfect. I had to read assignments three and four times to understand them. Warren taught me study skills that helped me break down and manage large amounts of information. I continued to have Warren test me for spelling long after it was required. I cannot imagine anyone loving high school as much as I did.

With a clear mental picture of what I wanted to achieve, I was able to stay focused and reach those goals. Sometimes, I surpassed them. In addition to being elected to the National Honor Society, I was the captain of three school sports teams. At 5 feet 9 inches tall and 175 pounds, I was not an imposing sports figure. I simply played sports with the same passion, perseverance, and resolve that I had for my studies. I have a strong kinesthetic intelligence. I love physical contact. I love competition and good sportsmanship. As a result of my efforts, I became a *Boston Globe* first-team All-Scholastic Fullback; I won the New England wrestling championship in the 165-pound weight class; and I was invited to a tryout with the New York Yankees.

At the University of Connecticut I met Dr. Hollis Fait, who was the first recipient of the Joseph P. Kennedy Foundation Grant. He was a prolific writer with many scholarly papers and several books on the subject of adapted physical education. Most important, he was passionate about children with disabilities, especially children with mental retardation. He was a beautiful blend of academics and love. I vividly remember traveling with Dr. Fait to the Mansfield Training School, an institution for individuals with mental retardation. When

Dr. Fait entered the children's ward, he was tackled by nearly 20 excited and happy children. Even the children who were blind found their way to Dr. Fait. They laughed, they kissed him, he tickled them, he laughed, and I was in awe. I remember thinking, "What a wonderful man. I want to be just like him."

It was because of Warren that I became a teacher. My father's condition and his struggle with it made me an adapted physical educator. Dr. Fait taught me how to truly love and enjoy teaching children with disabilities. Dr. Fait reached into my soul and touched the very essence of my spirit.

My first semester at Connecticut, I achieved a 2.85 grade point score and was awarded a scholarship. One of the happiest moments of my life was telling my parents they did not have to pay for my college education. My mother cried. The goals I set, my ability to love what I do, and my ability to remain focused, along with my innate desire to be successful, and my passion and perseverance literally paid off at the University of Connecticut. I played football and wrestled for all four years at UConn. I achieved Dean's List status my junior and senior years and finished with a 2.95 quality point average. It was now time to begin my career.

In 1970, I was hired to teach physical education at the elementary and junior high school level in Waltham, Massachusetts. I was also hired to start a wrestling program at Waltham High School. My life changed forever in September 1988 when I began teaching in Wayland, Massachusetts, and met Katie Lynch. Katie was born with a connective tissue disorder. She was 28 inches tall and her arms were 7 inches long. Although Katie was capable of walking short distances with the assistance of a custom built "mini" walker, she used a motorized wheelchair for mobility. In 1990, Katie and I worked six months to prepare for her version of the Walk for Hunger. She collected pledges that sponsored her by the foot instead of by the mile. She walked 200 feet and raised $1,700.00. When Katie graduated from Wayland High School she surprised her parents by walking across the stage to receive her diploma. We worked three months to prepare for that event. In April 2000, Katie walked the first 26.2 feet of the Boston Marathon to raise $28,000.00 for Children's Hospital in Boston. Katie trained six months and sustained several injuries preparing for this event. I was one of Katie's coaches for her marathon walk, and it was Katie who nominated me for the Disney American Teaching Award. Katie survived 13 life-threatening surgeries and was in constant pain before she died in October 2002. Katie was the epitome of mental toughness. Katie taught me that we are limited only by our thoughts and that the human spirit has unlimited potential. I bring this spirit to every part of my life, including my teaching. Katie has helped me to be patient, confident, and hopeful.

If you set goals, love what you do, stay focused, and pursue your dreams with passion and perseverance, your teachers will appear.

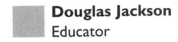
Douglas Jackson
Educator

D ouglas Jackson has been an educator for more than a quarter of a century, working with hearing impaired students for most of that time. You get the sense that he considers himself lucky to have had the opportunity to touch the lives of children who have this physical challenge; you never believe that he thinks they are lucky to have found him. His enormous enthusiasm for his work is somewhat surprising for a guy who has been teaching for more than 25 years. But when you talk to him, you know it's the real thing.

Jackson has been employed by the El Paso Regional Day School Program for the Deaf since 1995. He was recognized in 1994 by the Florida Law Related Education Association as its statewide Teacher of the Year, in 1998 as the statewide Deaf Education Teacher of the Year in Texas, and in 2000 as a Disney American Teacher Award honoree. He considers himself a work in progress. His purpose was and is to benefit and enrich the education of his gifted students. He doesn't see obstacles, only potential.

Douglas Jackson
Make the Connections Between
What Could Be and What Is

. . . it is true that all kids are like snowflakes and that no two children have identical gifts, talents, hopes, interests, and personalities.

S ometimes in a teacher's life it happens, moments when it all comes together. The planets line up, the basketball

---

Source: Printed with permission from George Douglas Jackson, teacher.

dances around the hoop before it plunges through, and a group of students soar out of the box together hand in hand.

I was fortunate enough to witness one such transcendent moment this past week when my fifth grade homeroom students delivered their PowerPoint presentation on the needs of deaf people in our system of justice to the assembled membership of the El Paso Bar Association. I mean, they were *signing it*, speaking it, role-playing it, living it, and nailing it. With wit, energy, enthusiasm, rubber faces capable of communicating a wide range of subtle nuances and determination, they marched onto this adult turf (a suit-and-tie luncheon at a posh restaurant) and by means of their presentation escorted the audience into their world, a world in which the constitutional and other legal protections afforded to deaf victims, defendants, jurors, and lawyers in what can be frightening and devastating legal situations are only as good as the communication bridges (especially interpreters) that are provided. And with this same wit, energy, talent, enthusiasm, and determination, they walked their audience back into their own world of writs and motions. They bowed toward an audience still laughing and still smiling, but also still absorbing what they had seen and heard . . . and, I hope, ready to make their corner of the world better and more accessible. That is the wonder of working with students like this. More about that in a moment; I am getting ahead of myself.

My name is Douglas Jackson. I am a teacher. I have always loved art, drama, language, learning new things, sharing ideas, and collaborating with like-minded people. I became a teacher because I knew that it could be the intersection of all of those interests and passions. In 1977 I was attending the University of Northern Colorado, where I was pursuing a degree in Social Studies Education and was beginning to see the light at the end of the tunnel. But I needed a place to live. At this time a group of UNC Deaf Education majors, having observed the way in which foreign language majors in language immersion dorms were benefiting from the opportunity to live, eat, breathe, and dream their respective languages 24/7, decided that the same approach might help them acquire sign language skills more naturally, comprehensively, and effectively. They rented a house and dubbed it "The Sign Inn." They only had one problem; they realized that they would have to advertise for one more housemate or they would never make that month's rent. Responding to that ad changed my life. A few years later I earned a Master's degree from the University of Rochester–National Technical Institute for the Deaf Joint Educational Specialist Program.

I began my trek up what would be a rather steep learning curve by teaching deaf high school students in Tallahassee, Florida. Our numbers were high because of the "Rubella Bubble." Many of my students had lost their hearing because they had contracted rubella as babies or because their mothers had contracted it during pregnancy. In 1985, I started taking courses in the education of the Gifted and Talented because I had students who qualified for both Deaf Education and GT services. When the "Rubella Bubble" burst and the number of hearing impaired students declined, I began to serve both populations. I found that the approaches and activities I used with gifted students often worked well with my deaf students (and vice versa).

A few words about deaf students. It is true that all kids are like snowflakes and that no two children have identical gifts, talents, hopes, interests, and personalities. But in addition to these traits, our students are unique in other ways. One student might have a severe loss; another, a profound one; still another, a progressive one. Some may struggle most with high frequencies, other with low frequencies. Some may lose their hearing after an early exposure to spoken language, while others are deaf from birth. We have students who wear hearing aids. We have students who have cochlear implants. The vast majority of our students are born into hearing families that are unprepared to communicate with them. Some families learn to communicate. Some do not. Consequently a lot of our students come into our program with linguistic and experiential deficits. Some no longer have the expectation that life is supposed to make any sense to them. Our job then is to shake them out of their passivity, reawaken their natural curiosity, and prove to them that this is indeed their world. But that something about the human spirit and the human heart that yearns to explore the world and communicate what it has learned, despite all of the obstacles that might be in their way, even if that spirit must develop its own approaches and tools for doing so. Many of my students are relentlessly curious and creative and have developed ways of understanding the outside world that are as individual as their own fingerprints. We don't have to teach these students to think outside of the box; they already do. Our job is to help them master the communication and academic skills they need to function both inside and outside of the box. Our job is to teach them to trust themselves, work hard, and make the connections between what could be and what is.

Over the years we have tried to do just that. I can't take credit for helping them find their way out of the box. I hope that I can continue to give them the skills and opportunities to make their world better, inside and outside of the box.

THE SCIENTISTS

Mario J. Molina
Nobel Prize Winning Chemist

In 1995, Mario Molina received the Nobel Prize in chemistry for his work in atmospheric chemistry and the effect of chlorofluorocarbons (CFCs) on the depletion of the ozone layer. He shared the Nobel Prize with F. Sherwood Rowland and Paul Crutzen. This was the first Nobel Prize awarded for research into the impact of man-made objects on the environment. The discoveries led to an international environmental treaty, which bans the production of industrial chemicals that reduce the ozone layer. He was named one of the top 20 Hispanics in Technology, 1998. He is one of the world's most knowledgeable experts on pollution and the effects of chemical pollution on the environment.

Presently, he is a Professor of Environmental Sciences at the Massachusetts Institute of Technology. According to Dr. Molina, " Although I no longer spend much time in the laboratory, I very much enjoy working with most graduate and postdoctoral students, who provide me with invaluable intellectual stimulus. I have also benefited from teaching; as I try to explain my views to students with critical and open minds, I find myself continually being challenged to go back and rethink ideas. I now see teaching and research as complementary, mutually reinforcing activities"

Mario J. Molina
It's OK to Be Original

Don't worry about doing something different. Just do it well.

I got hooked on science at a young age. Growing up in Mexico, I started reading biographies of famous biologists like Louis Pasteur; later I read about Albert Einstein. I received chemistry toys as gifts and became fascinated with them. The day I got my first microscope, though, was probably a key turning point. Antoni van Leeuwenhoek, the famous scientist and inventor, had some great ideas. The microscope was by far his best.

I remember sitting in my house with my new microscope and dropping a little dirty water onto a slide. What I saw, the movement of paramecia and bacteria, was the most fascinating thing I could ever imagine. What amazed me was the revelation that even if I couldn't observe something with my eyes, there was an instrument out there, right in front of me that could help me see it.

My curiosity was always fueled by the desire to find out how nature works. After high school, I attended the National Autonomous University of Mexico, where I received a bachelor's in chemical engineering. Then came a turning point in my life.

Source: Printed with permission from Professor Mario J. Molina.

For my master's I decided to study in Germany. The transition was tough. The people were much different, and the language was difficult to learn. But I persevered through the first year, a tough one, and eventually learned the language. Ironically, I learned German before I ever learned any English. In addition to having to learn German, learning the culture was just as tough. Even the way they taught–it was almost like they gave you a stack of books on the first day of your first semester, told you to read them all and come back for the last day of your last semester–was different from the North American style. I had the distinct feeling—and they had the unquestionable approach—that *I was on my own*. Eventually though, I did receive my master's in basic chemistry, and it came time for another tough decision.

Where would I go for my PhD? What I was really looking for now, even though my two degrees were in chemical engineering and basic chemistry, was a place where hands-on, basic science was taught. So I decided to move to the United States and attend the University of California at Berkeley. It turned out to be one of the wisest decisions I'd ever make.

The best lesson I learned at Berkeley was that science can be more fun and productive when working as a member of a team. Before Berkeley, my thinking was to do research on my own because it was fascinating to me. I wasn't thinking of the contributions I could make to better the world. When I was a kid back in Mexico, I had a lot of friends who didn't have the same ambitions I had. Many of them had what I would call an antischool bias. Their general idea was that it wasn't fun to do homework, study, or go to class. They thought that school just wasn't fun. Now don't get me wrong, I had fun with them, but they weren't thinking along the same lines as I was.

So as much as I loved research, I started understanding that science is teamwork. You enjoy doing science more when you share it with other people. Although it wasn't my immediate goal, I started realizing that the research I was doing was beginning to push the frontiers of science. I was starting to understand chemical lasers and how molecules function–aspects of science that were new and could be applied. That's when I turned my attention to environmental science–a science that could help benefit humanity as a whole.

After receiving my PhD, I decided to learn how the atmosphere functions. Before, as a chemist, I was simply looking into the nuances of chemical reactions; now, I had found a way to connect my life's work with reality. I moved to Irvine to team up with other scientists who were studying what happens to certain industrial compounds (most notably CFCs, or chlorofluorocarbons) once they are released into the atmosphere. Previous research teams had concluded that the CFCs were stable and thus would not be harmful to the environment. We challenged those assumptions and found that they would be destroyed in the stratosphere and eventually harm the environment. The question in the back of all our minds, "Will something happen to these compounds in the environment?," came into the forefront after our research. The answer was yes.

Based on our findings, we predicted that the ozone layer would be severely damaged. After international scientific research was conducted to test our theory, the answer came back. We were correct.

Of course, discovering something as potentially serious as a high-end environmental problem can be bittersweet. It's not as if we wanted something to be wrong, but we set out to find the facts, and we did. Now, steps are being taken to correct the problems that we found so the situation doesn't get worse. But had we never discovered how harmful CFCs could be, the hole in the ozone layer would still not be known.

The greatest piece of advice I can give anyone is not to be afraid to think outside the box. It's okay to be original. Don't worry about peer pressure. For me, science was and is great, and I don't mind being different. Don't worry about being different. Just do it well. When I think back to my childhood and my time growing up, I wonder if I would have been so successful had I not been different. My friends always thought that anything pertaining to school was not worth going through or working at or undertaking. For me, everything I wanted to do had something to do with school. Thankfully, I realized earlier that although my friends were important in social situations, I couldn't simultaneously succeed and succumb to peer pressure. If I wanted to make it in what I desired to do, I had to listen to my own heart. If I never followed my heart and learned science, I would have never been able to help the environment and the world. I never minded being different, and that's what has helped me succeed and achieve.

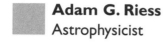

Adam G. Riess
Astrophysicist

*E*squire Magazine named him to its list of the "Best and Brightest of 2003," saying that this "world's foremost stargazer is fundamentally changing how we understand our universe—its age, its contents, its scope, and, most of all, its destiny. Meet the Edwin Hubble of our time."

Dr. Adam G. Riess is an associate astronomer at the Space Telescope Science Institute and an Adjunct Professor at the Johns Hopkins University in Baltimore, Maryland. Dr. Riess received his BS in physics from the Massachusetts Institute of Technology in 1992 and his PhD from Harvard University in 1996. Between 1996 and 1999 Riess was a Miller Fellow at the University of California at Berkeley. He joined the faculty of Space Telescope Science Institute in 1999.

In 1998, Dr. Riess published the first evidence that the expansion of the universe was accelerating and that it was filled with dark energy, a discovery that was called the Breakthrough Discovery of the Year by *Science* magazine that year. In 1999, he received the Robert J. Trumpler Award from the Astronomical Society of the Pacific for the doctoral thesis with the greatest impact in astrophysics. In 2000, *Time* named Dr. Riess one of hundred "Innovators of the Future," one of only six in the sciences.

Adam G. Riess
Knowledge ... the Great Equalizer

Curiosity and the ability to seek answers to your own questions is one of the most powerful tools you can have.

During long family drives when I was young, I would repeatedly ask my parents how much further it was to our destination. Growing tired of answering, they told me the number of the highway mile and thereafter I was content to estimate the distance and arrival time myself. Math, and later physics, excited me because they offered the power to figure out what I wanted to know on my own.

They say, "curiosity killed the cat," but don't believe it! Curiosity and the ability to seek answers to your own questions is one of the most powerful tools you can have. Knowledge and the ability to gather it is the great equalizer. You do not have to be rich or popular to be able to find things out or discover something new. It only takes curiosity and the courage to pursue the answers and an unyielding mind set to overcome the inevitable obstacles and challenges.

Physics, the subject that is central to my life's work started out as the hardest for me. When I first took physics in high school, I didn't understand it, and I needed help from a tutor. Then one day it just clicked. Physics was a new way of thinking and, once I started to think in this new way, I never stopped.

I also discovered that thinking about physics and the universe (and all the stars, galaxies, and planets in it) gave me a satisfying and global perspective about my life. In fact, when there was something in my every day life that was getting me down or troubling me, I found I could go out and look up at

---

Source: Printed with permission from Adam G. Riess.

the stars and my troubles began to feel insignificant. My Dad once told me that the stars were so far away that we only ever see them the way they were in the past since it takes millions of years for their light to get to us. I couldn't believe that they could be so far away! That cosmic perspective made me feel my individual problems were really small.

By the time I was a teenager I became curious about our whole universe. I wanted to know how old it is, where it came from, and whether it was getting bigger or smaller. I was amazed to learn in school that you could do more than just wonder about the universe. You could go out and measure it!

Astronomers used powerful telescopes and the same techniques that surveyors used to chart the changing expansion rate of the universe. I decided I wanted to help make the measurements necessary to answer my questions and discover how the universe was changing. Measuring the distance to far away galaxies in the universe, where there are no mile markers, is one of the biggest challenges in astronomy. In order to figure out how the universe was growing I needed to measure distances more than halfway across the universe!

In graduate school I developed a new method to make these measurements. My method was not as accurate as the mile markers on the highways but it was more accurate than previous methods.

When my teammates and I measured the rate at which the universe was growing, we found a big surprise! The universe is expanding faster and faster all the time! This was the opposite of what we and other astronomers expected we would see. Trying to understand why the universe is speeding up remains one of the biggest mysteries in science today. It's funny how you can set out to answer one question and end up raising another.

Vinton G. Cerf
Internet Cofounder and Developer

Vinton Cerf, one of the most celebrated technical architects of the last century, is Senior Vice President for Technology Strategy at MCI. In 1973 while working at Stanford University with support from DARPA (U.S. Department of Defense's Advanced Research Projects Agency) and in collaboration with Robert E. Kahn, Cerf developed the TCP/IP, the computer networking protocol that set the transmission standard for data communications on the Internet. In December 1997, President Bill Clinton presented the U.S. National Medal of Technology to Cerf and Kahn for founding and developing the Internet. In the course of his career, Cerf has received countless awards and commendations including the Marconi Fellowship, the Charles Stark Draper award of the National Academy of Engineering, the Prince of Asturias award for science and technology, and the Alexander Graham Bell Medal.

Cerf has been quoted as saying he was motivated in part by his significant hearing impairment to help devise and create the world's ultimate communications medium, the Internet. On the *Education Corner—For Kids Sake*, which is featured on Vint's Web site CerfsU (*www.mci.com/cerfsup*), Vint puts it this way, "I think one of the greatest gifts a parent can give a child is confidence in himself or herself. This may come in many forms—encouragement for constructive interests and creative work or demonstrating confidence in a child's judgment by allowing a child to make his or her choices in matters appropriate to age level and apparent maturity. . . . Above all else, kids need to know they are loved. Don't hesitate to tell them that warmly and often."

Vinton G. Cerf
Conventional Wisdom Is Not Always Right

A true visionary will see what others cannot or will not and will persist in the pursuit of that vision relentlessly, patiently, and endlessly.

There is an old expression, "Nothing succeeds like success!" I have always interpreted this to mean that once you are successful at anything, you have a "success" label stuck to you that will lead people to expect you to succeed in other ways and will give you liberty to reach for new goals. Even if these expectations and liberties are not well founded, they should not be ignored. They lead you to future opportunities and to new chances for more success.

Not every successful person will feel he or she has "thought outside the box." However, on careful analysis, it is often the case that a person's success can be attributed to a belief in achieving a goal that others thought impossible or imagining something that did not exist and then creating it.

It is sometimes joked that some remarkable achievements are a consequence of not knowing the task is "impossible" and going on to discover how to make progress. For many young people, this is a key to success. Absent conventional "wisdom" some very successful people simply plunge ahead, solving problems that crop up because they don't know or share the common belief that what they are attempting "can't be done."

When one realizes, for example, that the Wright Brothers were thought to be crazy because everyone knew that things that were heavier than air (unlike the hot air balloon) could not possibly fly, it should be clear that conventional wisdom

Source: Printed with permission from Vinton G. Cerf.

is not always right. Of course, this does not mean that it is always wrong. Gravity works and jumping off buildings because you think you can fly is probably a bad idea.

In the early 1970s, my colleague, Robert Kahn, began thinking about the ways in which computers communicated with each other. Each computer manufacturer (e.g., IBM, HP, Digital Equipment Corporation) had its own way of interconnecting its computers. These methods were not compatible, and it was unusual to find them part of the same network. A U.S. Defense Department project developed an example of a network that could interconnect these different computers; it was called the ARPANET, and it was based on the concept of "packet switching" (you can think of this as a kind of system of electronic postcards). It was considered a silly idea by conventional telecommunications engineers, but the project went on to show that this idea really could work.

The two of us teamed up in 1973 (having worked together before, along with many others, on the ARPANET). We quickly discovered that the problem of interconnecting heterogeneous packet networks had many constraints, so that eventually the basic design emerged as a consequence. Ultimately, we described the solution in a paper published in 1974 that outlined what became the TCP/IP protocol suite. Protocols are simply sets of conventions for computer communication. If everyone follows the rules, everyone could communicate effectively. We called the resulting system the Internet.

But that was just the beginning. Having envisioned the possibilities, it was now left to actually work out all the details and then, having done that on paper, actually implement the system through the writing of a good deal of software. We quickly found that testing the software for many computer systems revealed mistakes and problems in the basic design. So it was back to the drawing board for several iterations until a design seemed stable. The version of protocols used today on the Internet is the fourth iteration in the design (TCP/IP version 4).

People often ask, "Did you realize what would happen when you were working on the Internet so many years ago?" I wish I could say, "yes, I foresaw everything that has happened," but the truth is that we did not know at the time all the things that would later become possible. However, there were true visionaries who as far back as the early 1960s foresaw enough of what was possible to propose the design and construction of packet switched networks. While they did not see all the details, they saw enough of what might be possible to motivate themselves and others to explore this new space of ideas.

In the end, major successes almost always rely upon the commitment of many people. A true visionary will see what others cannot or will not and will persist in the pursuit of that vision relentlessly, patiently and endlessly. Indeed, I have learned from my own 30-year connection with the Internet that persistence counts. Although it was meant to be funny, there is a line in the popular movie, *Galaxy Quest*, that strikes me as relevant. The principal character in the film has a tag line, "Never give up!" and I think that sums up the life of person committed to a vision of what is possible.

Douglas C. Engelbart
Computer Scientist

Douglas Engelbart is a landmark figure in the history of computer science. He is best known as the inventor of the mouse. He is the founder and director of the Bootstrap Institute and has an unparalleled 30-year track record in predicting, designing, and implementing the future of organizational computing.

From his early vision of turning organizations into augmented knowledge workshops, he went on to pioneer what is now known as collaborative hypermedia, knowledge management, community networking, and organizational transformation. In addition to the mouse, his well-known technological firsts include display editing, windows, cross-file editing, outline processing, hypermedia, and groupware.

Engelbart's work has never been easy to grasp. Throughout the years he has been misunderstood, told he was "dead wrong," ridiculed, or simply ignored, which many say is to be expected when you are consistently 20 years ahead of your time. As each new wave of the computer revolution unfolds and experience catches up with Engelbart's vision, people come to understand what he was trying to accomplish.

After 20 years directing his own lab at SRI and 11 years as senior scientist, first at Tymshare and then at McDonnell Douglas Corporation, Engelbart founded the Bootstrap Institute, where he is working closely with industry and government stakeholders to launch a collaborative implementation of his work.

He has received countless awards, including the ACM Turing Award, the National Medal of Technology, the 1987 *PC Magazine* Lifetime Achievement Award, and the 1994 Price Waterhouse Lifetime Achievement Award. His big-picture vision, persistence, and pioneering breakthroughs have made a significant impact on the past, present, and future of personal, interpersonal, and organizational computing.

Douglas C. Engelbart
Imagine All Kinds of Things

What has kept me motivated and constantly pushing and advancing the industry of computer development, is that I know it is just the start.

My father died when I was nine. It was in the middle of the Great Depression. We lived out in the country near Portland, Oregon. This was the real country. I went to a small school. I helped milk the cow and tend the chickens and the garden. I played in the creek and in the forest behind our little farm. It was there that I was able to imagine all kinds of things.

I wanted to build an aircraft with a balloon and a propeller driven by a bicycle peddling arrangement. I spent countless hours unraveling burlap "Gunny" sacks; I would tie all the pieces together to make my own rope, for no practical reason at all. In those days I dreamed of inventing.

Being a shy kid, I didn't understand the social structures going on in school. I was so shy that I could have a locker next to someone for an entire year and not know or talk to the person. I don't know if I was motivated then. I think that came along later, when I became engaged to be married. I think that as I was growing up, the environment was shaping the way I thought.

Source: Printed with permission from Douglas Engelbart and Bootstrap Institute.

After graduating from high school in 1942, I went on to study electrical engineering at Oregon State University. After two years I was drafted into the Navy during World War II. I trained for a year as an electronic/radar technician and then served for a year in the Philippines. That was certainly an education for a country boy. From working with radar, I learned that you could display information on a screen. This information stayed with me, and I realized later that if radar equipment can do that, so could a computer.

After receiving my degree in electrical engineering in 1948, I settled on the San Francisco Peninsula as an electrical engineer at NACA Ames Laboratory, the forerunner of NASA. This was when my life's mission started to develop.

After several years there, I became engaged to marry a dream girl. Things were becoming important, so it was time to take my job more seriously. The next day, as I was driving to work, I visualized my expected career as a long hallway with nothing in it—it just went on and on. With nothing in the hall, it became clear to me that I had no real career goals. After thinking for a half an hour, I had an idea. I decided that I would create a career that maximizes its benefit to humanity. Now that I had decided on the focus of my career and what I was going to pursue, the next question was, "What was I going to do specifically?"

After three months, I concluded that organizing this great new career goal would create many complex problems for me, and I instantly realized that all of humanity would face challenges whose complexity and urgency would be increasing exponentially as society kept growing. I knew that these problems must be solved efficiently. I had hit the nail on the head. I would help people by finding a way to help them solve their complex problems ("augmenting the human intellect"). These big complex problems can only be solved by collective effort, so it will be very important to improve our collective capability for dealing with complex, urgent problems.

In 1951, I read a book called *Giant Brains, or Machines That Think* by Edmund C. Berkely and it seemed to open up a whole new path of knowledge. After thinking about it for several months, I decided computers would make a good lifetime focus. In those days, computers were called "magic brains."

As an electrical engineer, especially one trained to maintain radar equipment, I knew how electronics could put things on the screen. I knew if a computer could punch cards and print paper, then radar-like circuitry could let a computer print on a screen, and if radar equipment could respond instantly to an operator pushing buttons, then so could a computer, and if radar equipment could respond instantly to an operator pushing buttons, then so could a computer. I envisioned people sitting down in front of a screen and computers helping them solve their problems.

Computers were scarce then. In fact, I believe that there were just two in the country. I decided to get a graduate degree at the University of California at Berkeley, where they were at least building one computer. It was an uphill climb. My idea of "augmenting the human intellect," was not easily received. It was new and as with many new ideas, people were scared to go against what they knew. The turning point was 1963, when my research team and I were actively working towards problem-solvers using computer-aided working stations to augment their efforts. Some sort of device to move around the screen was needed. Thus the mouse was born.

We next moved on to building our own computerized working system for our research group to use. It could do word processing, e-mail, programming, etc., and provided much more flexible linking than even what the WWW (World-wide Web) does today. Then on to our involvement in the emergence and use of the Internet, initially called the Arpanet by Arpa, which involved the interlinking of computers.

What has kept me motivated and constantly pushing and advancing the industry is that I know it is just the start. Society is constantly advancing and changing. Problems are becoming more and more complex, and technology has to keep up with these changes. There's a lag time for people accepting new ideas. Although I have been working at "augmenting human intellect" for the last 50 years, I know that technology development is still at the beginning stages and there is so much to do, so my mission is just beginning.

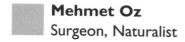
Mehmet Oz
Surgeon, Naturalist

Dr. Mehmet Oz is Vice Chairman of Surgery and Professor of Cardiac Surgery at Columbia University, Director of the Cardiovascular Institute, and Founder and Director of the Complementary Medicine Program at New York-Presbyterian Hospital. His research interests include heart replacement surgery, minimally invasive cardiac surgery, and health care policy. In addition to holding several patents, he has authored more than 350 publications, book chapters, abstracts, and books.

Dr. Oz received his undergraduate degree from Harvard University (1982) and a joint MD and MBA (1986) from the University of Pennsylvania School of Medicine and Wharton Business School. He was selected a Global Leaders of Tomorrow (1999) by the World Economic Forum and awarded the prestigious American Association for Thoracic Surgery Robert E. Gross Research Scholarship (1994–1996).

Dr. Oz is one of those rare out-of-the-box thinkers, who is also well rounded. He's a leader, inventor, scientist, and medical visionary who treats his patients medically *and* holistically. To bring his philosophy of "treating the whole patient" to the general public, Dr. Oz has appeared numerous times on all the major network morning and evening news and news magazine programs, as well as on PBS, CNN, the Discovery Channel, and Oprah.

Mehmet Oz
Persistent Curiosity

Even if I have to break rules, I keep looking.

As a five-year old, I used to slip behind the well-manicured gardens surrounding my grandfather's fish pool in Istanbul and watch the golden darts moving around just beneath the surface. I wanted to know the fish by touching, caressing, or maybe even squeezing them. Even then I was a tactile learner. One day, I remember reaching into the water to touch them, and then just a little deeper as they eluded me until I was submerged in refreshing fluid and dancing with the fish. They were gliding effortlessly and, as I looked toward the sun, I could see the glimmering surface of the water from below. Suddenly I felt cold and seemed heavier in the water. The surface seemed elusive as I kicked my feet ferociously and extended my hand until it disappeared above the water. Suddenly I felt pressure on my wrist and was jerked from the now scary water. My mother had not taken her eyes off her naughty and momentarily grateful son.

This true story is a metaphor for my life. First, I am persistently curious. I want to know more than allowed. Even if I have to break rules, I keep looking. The response "No" just means that I have to ask in a different way, even if sometimes I fall into the water. A failure, and more importantly, fear of failure has never stopped me from pursuing this goal. In heart surgery, when we lose a patient, the operator should return to the operating room as soon as possible to regain confidence.

Second, I seek differing perspectives on challenging topics. The easy solutions are frequently wrong and opportunity lies in understanding why seemingly mutually exclusive

Source: Printed with permission from Mehmet Oz.

paradigms are actually compatible. Seeing the water from above and below provided insights, albeit with potentially dangerous consequences. When I saw that my heart transplant patients required more than high-tech solutions, I began investigating alternative medicine at personal risk. Earnest endeavors are worth the danger because many will follow and benefit once the path is well lit.

Third, I keep my feet moving. In addition to propelling you out of difficult situations, you develop momentum that the undecided bystander can feel and support. When our first series of mechanical heart support patients were doing poorly, I kept searching for clues, even some that were outlandish, in order to stimulate proactive solutions.

Fourth, I am always grateful, ranging from my mother who saved me in the pool to my patients who continually provide me life lessons. I am grateful for my wonderful teachers who inspired me, talented teammates who build success with me, and loving family members who unconditionally support me. Being appreciative will beneficially influence the behavior of the people in your life and make folks want to spend time with you. And finally, you will find joy and happiness through gratitude, and this is the ultimate grading scale for success.

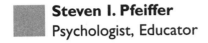

Steven I. Pfeiffer
Psychologist, Educator

Steven I. Pfeiffer is a Professor at Florida State University, where he directs the graduate program in mental health counseling. Prior to his appointment at Florida State, Dr. Pfeiffer served as Executive Director of Duke University's Talent Identification Program.

Dr. Pfeiffer received his PhD from the University of North Carolina in 1977. He is a licensed and board certified psychologist who served in the U.S. Naval Medical Service. He served as a clinical psychologist (reserves). Dr. Pfeiffer divides his professional time among teaching; researching and writing; test development; counseling children, adolescents, and families; and public speaking.

He is the lead author of the *Gifted Rating Scales*, a newly published test to identify multiple types of giftedness; the co-author of a book for parents, *Early Gifts: Recognizing and Nurturing Children's Talents*; a member of the editorial board of eight journals; and the author of almost one hundred scientific articles. Dr. Pfeiffer is a recipient of the Excellence in Research Award from the MENSA International Foundation.

Steven I. Pfeiffer
Let Your Dreams Evolve

. . . my family circumstances seem to set the stage. . . .

Even before the age of ten, I felt certain that I would one day be a pediatric cardiovascular surgeon. I was the first born to a second generation Jewish family of modest means.

Source: Printed with permission from Steven I. Pfeiffer.

My family lived in New York City, where my father worked as a salesman. No one before me in my immediate family had attended college.

When I was four, my younger brother was born with a life-threatening medical condition. My brother died only a few short years after his birth. Some of my earliest recollections are waiting patiently and alone outside of my brother's hospital room. What I recall with particular clarity are a few brief conversations with my brother's surgeon in the corridor of Mt. Sinai hospital. This recollection is vividly etched in my memory, undoubtedly because my parents imbued medicine, in general, and my brother's pediatric surgeon, in particular, with magical, even God-like qualities. Dr. Baronowski, my brother's primary physician, was—at least in the recesses of my early memory—a frequent topic of family discussion at the dinner table. As I look back on my childhood, my family circumstances seem to set the stage for my need to pursue a profession that would afford me the opportunity to help others.

While in college—during the turbulent 1960s—my interest in medicine waned and was preempted and transcended by a fascination with philosophy, sociology, and psychology. The often contentious and highly emotional era marked by campus peace demonstrations reinforced a growing personal interest in social and societal issues. I developed a close and special relationship with one college professor, Raymond Rainville, whose passion for psychology inspired in me a newfound intellectual interest and potential career track.

Dr. Rainville was one of the more popular professors on campus, in part because he was blind and yet in no way handicapped or disabled by his lack of sight. Ray was fresh out of graduate school, handsome, physically active, a bit cocky, and outspoken. He was a brilliant, provocative, and entertaining lecturer. I was intellectually enamored. During my senior year

I was privileged to take an independent study with Ray. We frequently met at his home and would stay up into the wee hours of the night discussing topics such as what makes us distinctly human, how can we reconcile living in the present when preoccupied with the past or future? Does the knowledge of our mortality provide us with motivation to seek meaning in our life? Is human nature basically deterministic, driven by irrational forces, unconscious motivations, and environmental contingencies or instinctual drives? Or are we free to choose and motivated by conscious goals and purposes?

My experience with Ray, my first true mentor, riveted my decision to become a psychologist. It has been more than 25 years since I completed my doctorate at the University of North Carolina-Chapel Hill. I have worked in a variety of settings and in a variety of capacities as a psychologist. I have served as a psychologist in the department of pediatrics at a tertiary care hospital, the director of a research and clinical training institute, on the faculty of a number of universities, and as a consultant to child guidance clinics, adolescent psychiatric hospitals, and public and private schools.

For the past five years, I have had the pleasure of serving as director of Duke University's internationally recognized program for gifted children (TIP). Over this quarter century, the profession of psychology has afforded me the personal satisfaction of working in a variety of settings as a health care professional. As a psychologist whose clinical work, teaching, and research has focused on children, youth, and families, I have been able to satisfy my early interest in working with a pediatric population and my later-developed interest in focusing on the psychological, social, and existential rather than medical. In other words, I've dealt with the issues that children most often face.

THE ATHLETES

Rod Gilbert
Ice Hockey All-Star

R od Gilbert is an outstanding example of a person who overcame almost insurmountable odds to become successful in his chosen profession–one of the top right wingers in National Hockey League history. Rod Gilbert was a consistent scorer during an excellent NHL career with the New York Rangers that lasted 18 seasons and, although he never played on a Stanley Cup champion team, he was often at his best in the postseason.

Born on July 1, 1941, in Montreal, Gilbert progressed through minor league hockey to star as a junior in Guelph, Ontario. It was during a junior game that he skated over a piece of debris and suffered a broken back. Gilbert almost lost his left leg, and it took two operations to correct the damage.

Gilbert finally made the team outright at training camp in 1962. He was blessed with a hard shot that often dipped, and he didn't shy away from battling hard in the corners or in front of the opposition net. Although he was only 5 foot 9 inches and 175 pounds, Gilbert was an excellent skater and puck handler, who went on to play almost 16 full seasons in the NHL—all as a New York Ranger. In that time, he set or equaled 20 team scoring records and when he retired in 1977, Gilbert trailed only one other right winger—Gordie Howe— in total points.

In 1976, Gilbert was awarded the Masterton Trophy, which is awarded annually to the player "who best exemplifies the qualities of perseverance, sportsmanship and dedication to hockey." Gilbert was immortalized in New York hockey history, when his #7 was raised to the Garden's rafters on October 14, 1979. IIe is one of three players in the history of the New York Rangers to have received that honor. He was elected to the Hockey Hall of Fame in 1982.

Rod Gilbert
Go the Extra Mile

There are always going to be stumbling blocks along the way. Don't let that stop you.

L ife is like a big wheel: when you give, you get back much more in return. You don't always get it back from the person you gave to, but the act of giving seems to follow you in life, and what you get back is far more than you ever expected or imagined.

As I look back over the course of my life, I attribute my success as a NHL hockey player and as a person to a number of things, including the giving and generosity of others. My family, my brothers, and the countless people I have met have all fueled me in achieving my goals one way or another.

Source: Printed with permission from Rod Gilbert, New York Rangers Hockey Hall of Famer.

When I pass along my thoughts and perspectives as to what motivated me to reach my personal pinnacle of achievement, the first things I emphasize are *love* and *passion*. First, you have to find something that you *love*—dancing, music, hockey—and be *passionate* about it. Dream about it. Choose a role model who has "made it." Go to the source and find out about that person's experience.

If it's music that you love, find the music teacher in your school. You must ask questions. With the Internet today, research is so much easier than when I was a kid. Once I knew what I wanted to do, I asked questions, read countless books on hockey, and I talked to other hockey players. I asked myself, "How did the last great hockey player do it?" and then I found the answers. It helped me to develop my initiative to succeed. My hero was Boom Boom Geoffrion. Go the extra mile to get the answers and live your dream.

It's all gradual: you have to pay your dues through your attention, and practice. If you truly love something it's not a sacrifice or a chore. It wasn't hard for me to play hockey at 20° below. You must go the extra mile to get the answers. You must live your dream!

Once you've done all that, immediate success is not assured. It's just the beginning. You must work hard, and you have to pay your dues. By asking your own questions, you will find out what you need to do to be great. You will find out all those "supposed" sacrifices. You can't get discouraged if you are not an immediate star, you can't get discouraged if you not good at it. If you want it, never give up. Never give up, go for it; go for it! Tell yourself, "I can do it, I can!" You may not end up a hockey star, but this quality of perseverance will serve you well in life and will be pivotal in something else you accomplish.

"Never give up" are the words that have been running through my head my whole life. With those words in my head, I succeeded in becoming one of the best players in Canada.

With those words in my head, I made it through a broken back, being paralyzed for two months, and the possible amputation of my leg.

When I was 19 and playing junior hockey in Guelph, Ontario, I unfortunately skated over an ice cream wrapper that a fan threw on the ice. I was skating at full speed and I tumbled across the ice and slammed into the boards. The result of the fall was devastating. They rushed me to the Mayo Clinic in Minnesota for two months. They took a bone out of my tibia to fuse my back. In those months at the Mayo clinic, I developed a severe staff infection. One day, my mother came into my hospital room crying with the news that they wanted to amputate my leg. I told my mother with total confidence, "they're crazy. I'll be fine. I'll never give up. " There was so much yet to accomplish.

Along the way there are always going to be obstacles. In my case, the obstacle was physical injury. There are always going to be stumbling blocks. Don't let that stop you. Don't let these inevitable barriers slow you down. When I suffered an injury, any injury, large or small, I thought to myself, "Okay this is my turn. Injury is part of the game. Okay, I'll get better." I knew I was fortunate and I was honored to be doing what I was doing.

Another lesson that I have learned is never to let other kids break your spirit. I started playing hockey very young, and much of the time I played with older kids. Older kids can hurt your confidence. Other kids are not going to recognize your "greatness." I was lucky enough to have had two older brothers there to protect me—especially my older brother John. But even if you don't have older brothers, stand tough and understand that this happens to all kids—it's not just you. Little by little you gain your confidence. It's not easy.

There are going to be obstacles, hindrances, barriers, and injuries all along the way. When I first got to the junior league,

I spoke French and no English. All the instructions were in English. I didn't understand anything. My teammates made fun of me. I quickly learned the English words "same thing." If someone asked me what I wanted, I would point to another player and in English say "same thing." It didn't matter. Nothing mattered. I was doing something that I loved.

I kept going until the New York Rangers summoned me from the Kitchener-Waterloo Eastern Pro League club during the Spring of 1962. They wanted me to participate in a playoff series against Toronto. In my first game, I scored two goals and an assist, and the following season I was a regular member of the New York Rangers. In my first season with the Rangers, I scored 31 points. I was suffering with back pain from my injury, but I kept trying and going. In the next two seasons, I scored 64 and 61 points, which were respectable numbers. Then, after fighting through back pain in the 1966 season, it was decided that I should undergo a second spinal fusion.

I died in my bed during a visit from my coach Emile Frances. I was gone for maybe three or four minutes, and I left my body. It was an amazing experience. I looked down from above the bed, and I saw them working on me, trying to restore my heartbeat. My coach was there and when the nurse said that they thought they lost me, I heard the coach say to bring me back because I was his best right winger. And somehow they brought me back.

I played the following season and the Rangers went to the playoffs. I never gave up and I kept going. In the 1971–1972 season, I reached the pinnacle of my career when I scored 43 goals and tallied 54 assists on my way to the all-NHL First-Team and an All-Star selection. The G-A-G (Goal-A-Game) line, which included Jean Ratelle, Vic Hadfield, and me, finished third, fourth, and fifth that season in scoring and led the Rangers to the Stanley Cup finals.

In the 16 full seasons with New York, through hard work and determination, I broke 20 club scoring records, registered 16 shots on goal in a single game, and when I retired with 406 goals and 1021 points, I was second in scoring among all right wingers in the history of the game, right behind the great Gordie Howe. I never gave up. I loved what I was doing. I kept working and trying.

No two kids are the same. Each one has a determination and passion for what he or she wants to do. It is a sacrifice for parents to help their children identify their passions. It's an effort to take kids early in the morning to hockey practice, or any other lesson. Yet it is these things that will help your children develop and learn life-defining skills. They will learn to win and to lose; they will learn lessons that will partner them throughout their lives.

Brian Martin
Luge Olympic Medalist

B rian Martin is a young man who has dedicated himself to working hard. He doesn't feel he is exceptionally better athletically than his friends or other athletes, but he knows what his goal is, and he knows he has to work harder than everyone else to reach it.

Since the inception of the U.S. Luge Association in 1979, the U.S. Luge Team has skyrocketed to world-class competitor status, winning more than 300 international medals. As a member of the most successful doubles team in U.S. luge history, Brian Martin and his partner Mark Grimmette have captured 9 world cups and 39 international medals. In addition to their 2 Olympic Medals—silver in 2002 and bronze in 1998— they have raced to 3 overall world cup titles, 2 Challenge Cup Crowns, and 2 World Championship bronze medals.

They are now working on building momentum toward a gold medal finish in the 2006 winter games in Turin, Italy. It's what he's worked for, it's what he has devoted his life to, and he is determined to accomplish this goal.

Brian Martin
Unyielding Devotion and Dedication

I don't win races because I am a superman, it is all the hard work and determination that got me there.

I don't see myself as an extraordinary person. What I have accomplished may be extraordinary. I have been to the Olympic Games twice and have come away with a medal

---

Source: Printed with permission from Brian Martin.

both times. Luge is the sport that I have dedicated my life to. It may be a simple sport—get on a sled and go down the hill and the fastest to the bottom wins. But it definitely did not come easily or without a lifetime of dedication and relentless effort.

I grew up in Palo Alto, California, where I was just like every other kid in town. I was involved in a lot of sports just like all of my friends. I played soccer well, but I wasn't Pélé. I swam fast, but not as fast as the other guy. I made a few spectacular catches out in right field, but at the plate no one feared me. I didn't fit the mold for cross-country, but I was still a fast runner. What is most important is that I enjoyed participating in a lot of sports, irrespective of whether I excelled in them or not. I was never the best guy out there, but I was in the game, and I always had fun.

I have been sliding for over half of my life, and I have won countless races, in addition to taking several titles. Winning a medal in the Olympics is certainly exceptional. But what I find equally significant and extraordinary is the unyielding devotion and dedication required to reach my "personal best" in the sport of luge.

I have spent so much time dedicated to the sport, I often think to myself, "How many runs have I taken? How many pounds have I lifted? How many hours have I trained?" To be quite honest, I don't know. We train eleven months of the year and half of that time there are no tracks in the world open for us to *slide on*. For a good part of that time, I am in the weight room just waiting for the winter to come so it will get cold enough *for ice*. All summer it is lifting, jumping, throwing, and running. It takes years to get into shape and even longer to learn the game.

When people see the Olympics every four years, I often get the feeling that they think the athletes are at the games because we were all born with some extra, super gene that has transformed us into something beyond human, quite possibly bordering on superhuman, and even more extreme, the athletic "freaks of nature." I have to laugh to myself. It just isn't true. I'm still the guy that goes mountain biking with my friends, Will and Dave, who love to boast about how easily they kick my butt!"

I don't win races because I am a superman, it is the all the hard work and determination that got me there. That doesn't mean that there are no mistakes to be made and lessons to be learned. I have learned some hard lessons over the years. For example, in the technical area of the sport, when it is colder than minus ten degrees Celsius it is better to run sharper runners, so that you will keep control of the sled, not the rounder runner, which is faster. The sharper runner offers more control so you can keep off the walls at seventy miles an hour. Sometimes you just don't go only for the speed; it's the skill and training that are important.

With good coaches and sharp listening skills, you don't have to learn all of the lessons the hard way. I have learned to get the most I can from the skilled professionals around me. I have been lucky. I have been surrounded by a strong support system. My coach has taught me about the art of sled building, he knows more about how to tune and finesse speed out of a sled than I can ever hope to.

The sport of luge has taught me so much. Along with this intensive learning process, one develops many personal goals. One goal that is written in stone and I live by every day, is to learn something new everyday, on or off the track.

Luge has given me the opportunity to travel around the world. My first trip to Europe with the luge team was in 1990. Our first track was in Sigulda, Latvia. This was when Latvia was a part of the Soviet Union. We had to fly through Moscow. It was an eye opening experience. We walked through the shops and there was nothing to buy, whole department stores with bare shelves and people milling around hoping that there would be something that they needed. I have not only learned about the sport of luge, but I have learned about the world.

Because of the hard work and intense effort of an everyday guy (that being me), I have learned many valuable life lessons, including how to go fast and how to be a better person. These are two totally different lessons, but both being important to *who I am* as a person, and what *I do* as an athlete.

I feel blessed that I have had the opportunity to follow my dreams and compete in luge for so many years. I know that it has not only been my dedication that has earned me spots on two Olympic teams, but the lessons learned from my teammates and coaches that has helped me reach my personal pinnacle of success. Not all that I have learned has been on the track.

The world is a big place and luge has given me the opportunity to see a small slice of it. It has opened my eyes to what is out there. I am certainly not done yet, and I still have more to learn. The one thing I am sure of is that I am going to take all that I have learned, along with the need to achieve, and go out there, work hard, and win races.

Rachael Scdoris
Iditarod Sled Dog Musher

When she described society's attempts to pigeonhole her, Rachael Scdoris stated emphatically that she never was going to be the stereotypical girl who is blind. In Rachael's voice was a determination to lead more than a regular life!

Rachael Scdoris is a 19-year-old legally blind sled dog musher from Bend, Oregon. She was born with a rare vision disorder known as congenital achromatopsia, which causes nearsightedness, farsightedness, and colorblindness. She has just recently earned the right to fulfill her dream of competing in the 2005 Alaskan Iditarod by placing sixth in the 400-mile John Beargrease Marathon Race. This was the second of two highly respected Iditarod qualifying races that Rachael had to complete to qualify for the 1,200-mile Iditarod. Rachael will make sports history as the first legally blind athlete to ever compete in the Iditarod.

To do so she had to win approval for special accommodations that allow her to safely compete. Rachael will run the 1,200 mile continuous race in March 2005 with a visual interpreter, who driving a second dog team and communicating via two-way radio, will ride ahead of Rachael to warn her of obstacles, such as low hanging branches, broken ice, and even moose on the trail.

Besides being a highly skilled sled dog racer, Rachael Scdoris is a fiercely competitive long-distance track and cross-country runner. Rachael earned a varsity letter in high school and was ranked third nationally in both the 1,500 and 3,000 meters by the U.S. Association of Blind Athletes.

Rachael's story of hope, courage, and determination to overcome obstacles has attracted national attention. Rachael has been formally honored by several organizations, including the Women's Sports Foundation, the Oregon Commission for the Blind, and Goodwill Industries of California. In focusing only on the possibilities, she's a role model to everyone, not only to people who are blind.

Rachael Scdoris
Ignore What Others Say, Do What You Love

I wouldn't even consider giving up, or quitting. Those concepts are not available to me, they are not in my vocabulary, and they are not an option.

February 26, 2004. I am 19 years old as I write this narrative to all the parents, teachers, and kids reading this book. I have my entire life ahead of me. I feel that most of the goals, which seemed to many as merely a child's fantasy just a few years ago, are now well within my reach as I approach early adulthood. When I was only 8 years old, I told my father I was going to run the great Alaskan Iditarod someday. The Iditarod is the 1,200-mile sled dog race held in Alaska each year. It is the ultimate test of human and canine endurance.

This dream of *running* the Iditarod may seem ambitious for any child at 8 years old, but for me, most thought the undertaking was insurmountable. I was born legally blind and with it came all the challenges associated with my daily reality.

When I was 4 years old, I was given my first white cane. The person who was training me to use the white cane, or "the blind stick" as I called it, insisted that it would give me freedom and mobility. If I learned to use it correctly, I was told I would be able to cross streets all alone and do all sorts

---

Source: Printed with permission from Rachael Scdoris.

of wonderful things. Magic powers were attributed to my "blind stick!" I was told that people would recognize me as a blind child and would stop their cars and let me cross the street. I can guarantee you that people did not stop and let me cross the street. I don't think they even noticed my cane. If they did, they either didn't know what it was or they simply didn't care.

I didn't really know that I was that different until third grade. Before third grade I had the cane and the glasses as well as the binoculars that I used to see the board, but it was in third grade that the other kids made me feel that I was different.

At times other kids got me down. I felt as if they viewed me as the little blind nerd, a role I was not going to accept. But the challenges that I experienced during that time have served me well and have been inspirational in the way I look at life. I never liked being thought of as the blind kid, so in middle school, I pushed myself to become an athlete.

After going through years of kids teasing me and the occasional teacher who was uncaring or insensitive, I developed my never give up philosophy of life. When I was 15, I finished the 13-day 536-mile Wyoming Stage Stop Sled Dog Race.

I have run the 300-mile AttaBoy 300 race three years in a row. Most recently, I ran the 350-mile Race to the Sky in Montana and the 400-mile John Beargrease Marathon Sled dog race in Montana. I am now one of the top sled dog racers in the world. I wouldn't even consider giving up, or quitting. Those concepts are not available to me. They are not in my vocabulary, and they are not an option.

People ask me if I ever get frightened when I am racing, and I say no, that's not what I'm feeling. I guess it's stress that I feel—the stress of the competition, the stress of the race. Recently my lead dog took off down a train track while I was in the midst of the race. That was stressful, but it's all part of it.

My next race is next January, but I will start training in September. My next step is also college, but I don't know what I will be studying. The one thing I am sure of is that I found something in my life that I am passionate about.

Both my parents have been great and have offered me support. If I had any advice to offer parents, I would refer to my parents as role models. Parents encourage your kids, let them know you love them, and give them what they need when they need it.

To kids my advice is simple: Find something that you love to do, and if the other kids are unkind and callous, just ignore them. Take it from me; eventually they will grow out of it.

Tori Murden McClure
Rower, Skier, Mountain Climber

Tori McClure was born on March 6, 1963, in Brooksville, Florida, but she spent much of her childhood in Pennsylvania and went to high school in Louisville, Kentucky, where she currently resides with her husband Mac. Tori attended Smith College and while she was there she played four years of varsity basketball, learned to cross-country ski, and learned to row.

In college, Tori had planned to attend medical school, but a tragic incident late in her junior year caused a change of mind. After graduation Tori traveled to Alaska and spent a summer in the wilderness kayaking, backpacking, and climbing. When she returned to civilization she earned a Master's at Harvard Divinity School.

During her last year of divinity school, Tori took two and a half months off from school to ski 750 miles across Antarctica to the geographic South Pole. She and another woman were the first women to reach the South Pole by an overland route. She returned to Harvard and wrote her thesis comparing the rigors of the backcountry adventure with "the far more rigorous" urban adventure. After divinity school, Tori ran a shelter for homeless women. Watching the mayhem in the lives of her clients spurred Tori to continue her studies by attending law school at the University of Louisville.

While Tori was in law school she tried out for the U.S. Olympic Rowing Team, but an automobile accident on the way to the Olympic trials destroyed her hope of making the team. She returned to law school and took a job working for the Mayor of Louisville in the area of public policy. She passed the bar exam the summer after graduation and soon she was in search of another challenge.

She heard about a rowing race across the Atlantic Ocean. In her first attempt, she was hit by Hurricane Danielle. She was injured, and her boat was damaged. She went home and took a job working for the famous boxer Muhammad Ali. On September 13, 1999, Tori made her second attempt to row across the Atlantic. She left from Africa, and on December 3, 1999, she landed on the other side of the ocean on the island of Guadeloupe. Finally, she was the first woman to successfully cross the Atlantic in a rowboat.

Tori Murden McClure
Patience, Endurance, Resourcefulness

The impossible just takes a little longer.

I grew up with a mentally handicapped brother, along with a sense of helplessness and a desire to want to make things better, make things different, make things okay for those who are different. I was raging against the wind in the sense of really wanting to make things better for a lot of folks. Life really isn't fair for everyone. For some of us it is, for some of us it's more than fair, and I felt that I could make things better by doing things people admire, and some of the things that are admired by people are embraced for fairly odd reasons . . . like rowing a boat across the Atlantic Ocean.

My favorite quotation comes from Theodore Roosevelt, who said, "Far better it is to dare mighty things, to win glorious triumphs, even though checkered by failure, than to rank with those poor spirits who neither enjoy much nor suffer

Source: Printed with permission from Tori Murden McClure.

much because they live in the gray twilight that knows neither victory nor defeat."

The truest challenges for humanity are not found in the wilderness; they are found in civilization. My hope is that my adventures have taught me the patience, endurance, and resourcefulness necessary to take on far more important challenges. Challenges like ignorance, poverty, racism, and despair.

In my quest to make things better and different, I went from one driven element to the next driven element, and it was education that opened the doors to all my opportunities. My educational experiences have taught me to believe in the saying "The impossible just takes a little longer."

No one can guess where the things you are learning now will take you in the future. I learned to cross-country ski at Smith College on a pair of skis I purchased from a graduating senior for $25.00. In 1989, I skied across the continent of Antarctica to the geographic South Pole. I learned to row at Smith. In 1999, I rowed a boat solo and unassisted across the Atlantic Ocean.

I tried out for the U.S. Olympic team as a rower and didn't make it. Then, I saw this flyer about this rowing race across the Atlantic and, I thought, ahhhh, this is the race for me, because I can go for ever—I'm just not particularly fast over short distances. It didn't work out terribly well: it was a two-person race, and I had revolving partners. My eventual partner was not really an athlete and was not versed in facing hardship. We made it about 90 miles off shore, and our electrical system crashed, forcing us to come back.

Things did not turn out as planned, and we were not able to complete the race. I returned to work fixated on the premise of crossing the Atlantic in a rowboat. "I told hundreds of school children that I was going to row across the Atlantic." A year passed and a watch company in Italy called me offering to sponsor me if I would attempt to row solo and without assistance across the Atlantic Ocean.

In my first attempt, I was trying to row from west to east. I rowed 3,400 miles before I was hit by Hurricane Danielle. I was no match for the waves of the storm. During the hurricane, my boat capsized 13 times in the course of a single day and the next day the boat capsized some more. One capsize dislocated my shoulder and the next one popped it back into place. The boat also flipped *end* over *end* twice: For the boat to flip in that direction, the waves have to be twice as tall as the boat is long. My boat was 23 feet long and 6 feet wide at the water line, with a little cabin in the stern. The entire boat weighed about 2,000 pounds, meaning the waves that capsized me had to be at least 50 feet high.

There was one time when I thought to myself, "This is the end." I went out intending to set off my distress beacon, which I deliberately put along the bow bulkhead so I couldn't just set it off in a raving panic as I could if it were in the cabin. I really had to think about whether I wanted to set it off and, if I decided to do it, then I wanted to have to work hard at it. I got out of the cabin and crawled across the deck to get to the Emergency Position Indicating Radiobeacon (EPIRB), a device designed to save your life by identifying that you are in distress and giving your location. But during the time it took for me to get out there, crawl across the deck, and get hold of the distress beacon, I recognized that I really couldn't ask another human being to come out into that storm to get me. So I tied the distress beacon to my life vest and went back inside the cabin, fully expecting to die. But by God, I wasn't going to have someone else killed rescuing me.

This was my responsibility. I put myself in the middle of the Atlantic. Nobody forced me to go out there, and I wasn't out there earning a living, fishing, or running a cruise ship. I was in a rowboat, and I chose to be there. So I went through five or six more capsizes that day with a distress beacon in one hand, and another hand that would not push the button. There were times when I wanted to die. I thought, "Let's just get this over with because I can't take the terror." Yet there were other times I thought that I really wanted to live. But finally I made it home.

After my first attempt, I went home disheartened. I found a job working for the famous boxer Muhammad Ali. As I was sitting with Muhammad eating lunch, he looked across at me and said, "Were there ever times when you were out there and you wondered, 'why am I here?'" I looked back at him and responded, "Muhammad, were there times when you were out in the boxing ring and asked yourself, 'Why am I here?'" He looked at me and just laughed. Through the months of working with Ali, I learned some significant lessons. As I studied the life of Muhammad Ali, I realized that "a failure is not a person who falls; a failure is a person who falls and does not try to get up again."

On September 13, 1999, the day of my second attempt to cross the Atlantic in a rowboat, I left from an island off the coast of Africa. On December 3, 1999, I landed on the other side of the ocean on the island of Guadeloupe. Going from east to west, I felt that I was rowing a kinder and gentler part of the ocean than on my first try. Not once did I get the feeling that I wasn't going to make it. Not once did I get that feeling of terror that I had experienced during my first attempt.

The big fear on the second trip was Hurricane Lenny and not knowing how bad the storm was going to be. The storm kept turning back and forth, but by the time it came directly over my boat, it had lost its teeth. It was barely of tropical storm force, as the waves were roughly half of those of Danielle. But sitting out there listening to the weather report, there was no way for me to know if the storm was going to hit me or if I was going to make it. I was absolutely petrified.

I found myself thinking, "I cannot go through another hurricane in a rowboat. I just can't do it."

During the second row, the experiences may have been similar to the first, but I knew how to make it different. I was reacting out of my heart rather than my head and came away thinking that in the beginning I was searching for enlightenment.

I came home recognizing that if there was going to be enlightenment for me, it wasn't going to be intellectual. It would always be a matter of heart. I could not have made it to where I am today without some wonderful support systems. I was fortunate enough to have had wonderful teachers who filled the surrogate parenting role, considering I came from the All-American dysfunctional family. At every fork in the road, I had some magical mentor. Usually it was a teacher who made the difference.

I'm on to a new chapter in my life, although not as physical as before. I'm now focusing on other challenges, along with being married to the most wonderful man in the world. I'm putting the physical challenges on hold for a while, although I'm set to climb Mt. McKinley in June. Okay, so maybe not all the physical challenges.

Fred Zimny
U.S. National and Olympic Luge Team Manager

Regardless of the weather, if you are interested in trying out for the USA Olympic Luge Team, the first face you will see is Fred Zimny. Zimny, voted the *US Olympic National Development Coach of the Year*, lives up to that title and more. He has traveled over 150,000 miles looking for the next U.S. Olympic Luge hopeful, trying out countless kids between the ages of eleven and fourteen on a simulated sled with wheels. When you look at him you see an encouraging, disciplined, and focused presence in search of kids with possibility.

Fred Zimny was a member of the U.S. National Luge Team from 1979–81 and was the U.S. Team's men singles alternate in the Lake Placid 1980 Winter Olympics. Always actively involved in supporting the U.S.A. Luge effort, he not only became a head coach of the U.S. Luge Association in 1987, a position which he still holds, but he has also been the U.S. Recruitment and Development Manager since 1993.

As team leader for the U.S. Olympic Luge Team in 1998 and 2002, his commitment to the sport accompanied the U.S. Olympic Team to the Winter Olympics in Nagano, Japan and Salt Lake City, Utah.

If your child has what it takes to fly down an icy track on his or her back, with control and perseverance, look for Fred Zimny at the tryouts; with almost thirty years of sliding experience under his belt, he can spot talent.

Fred Zimny
Unconditional Support

. . . an outlet for self-expression that will truly allow them a unique experience. . . .

Kids can generally be divided into two groups when it comes to self-expression: those who just want to fit in with the rest of the crowd and those who try to set themselves apart from everyone else. This is most evident in the activities that kids choose to participate in, particularly when it comes to sports. The traditional sports of baseball, football, and basketball have long been the activities of choice for kids seeking a competitive outlet in an "all-American," yet conventional, way.

More recently, "extreme" sports have come into vogue, thanks to their individualistic appeal and mass saturation (and marketing) by the media and corporate America. Ironically, these sports that were once considered fringe and radical have now become mainstream. Who would have thought that BMX racing would make it into the Summer Olympics?

But there are still many sports and activities available to kids who crave an outlet for self-expression that will truly allow them a unique experience—sports where the obscurity of the activity is part of the attraction. Distance running, short track speed skating, Frisbee golf, biathlon, soapbox derby racing, and kayaking are good examples. In my case, it was luge.

Luge is about as far as you can get from a traditional American sport. While it doesn't rival the popularity of skiing in Europe, the most successful athletes there still enjoy a high degree of notoriety (and financial gain). In the United

---

Source: Printed with permission from Fred Zimny.

States, this is not quite the case. For example, how many Americans know that the United States has won four medals in luge in the last two Olympic Winter Games, or that the United States has won 306 medals in international competitions since the 1994 Olympics? In my case, the attraction was the possibility of Olympic competition and everything it represented. I was a 15-year old sophomore in high school when luge first sparked my interest. It had everything I was looking for as a kid whose first love was auto racing. It had the speed, competition, possibility for success, and most of all, a uniqueness that would set me apart from everyone else.

I was lucky because I had the unconditional support of my father. In the years to come, he would be the reason for my continued involvement in the sport. It is now almost thirty years later, and I am still involved in it. My father was the one who woke up at 4 AM to drive for two hours, three days a week to the West Point Military Academy, so I could work out on what was then the cutting edge of fitness equipment. He was the one who constructed an indoor start ramp down the hallway of our house and into the kitchen so I could practice luge starts indoors when the weather was bad. And it was my dad who answered the 3 AM phone calls from Europe when I was excited about buying my first sled.

This support and a modest degree of success as a National Team member and the alternate on the 1980 U.S. Olympic Team sowed a passion that would continue to burn in me even to this day.

As the current U.S. National and Olympic Team Manager, I still get excited before every race at the possibilities and struggles that lie ahead. I still love the sound of a sled gliding by at more than 80 mph as the steel runners cut into the ice surface. I am still filled with anticipation at the first snowfall of the year knowing that the upcoming luge season is not far behind. These along with once in a lifetime experiences like marching into the Opening Ceremonies for the 2002 Winter Olympic Games with the U.S. Team, an Olympic Games on U.S. soil just months after September 11, serve to keep my passion for luge alive.

As coaches, it's up to us to help inspire our athletes with a similar passion and to help them identify the sport or activity that motivates them to success. To some, success might mean being a starting player for their soccer team for the first time, to others it could mean winning an Olympic medal for the United States or winning the Indianapolis 500.

No matter what the activity, kids should be encouraged to pursue the interest of their choice with the guidance, support, and constructive criticism of parents and coaches. It may not be the activity we would have chosen for them but in the end, they'll stick with it because it's *their* passion.

The Source Book:
Exceptional
Programs,
Adventures,
and Voyages for
Your Child

AGES YOUTH TO COLLEGE

Wonderful programs and experiences are available to children today. This directory presents a sprinkling of significant programs around the country. It provides the parent, teacher, and child with a place to begin. It is a balanced list, in terms of program selection and geographic location. The programs were chosen and researched thoroughly. All of them have been contacted and/or visited by our staff or noted camp and program consultants.

Program selection and evaluation is not an exact science; phone numbers, fees, and course outlines can change with time. This directory is intended as an overview of the types of programs offered across the country and, as a result, it is not a complete listing. This index serves to enlighten parents to the different programs available for their children. It is for the child who wants to explore new horizons and different experiences, and for parents who want to embrace and support the unique interests of their children.

The programs are organized according to various personality traits, qualities, and attributes. These headings were designed to define the persona of each child. If your child is a leader, you will find appropriate programs listed in the category entitled "Leader, Negotiator, Debater, Peacemaker". The programs in this category will complement the child who might be a future president, international affairs expert, attorney, or corporate head. Alternatively, if your child's social conscience is dominant, the programs listed under "Altruist, Community Servant, Healer, Teacher" may catch your eye.

PROGRAMS: By Sphere of Interest

Altruist: Community Servant, Healer, Teacher
Artist: Musician, Performer

Athlete: Competitor
Designer: Architect
Entrepreneur: Financier, Economist
Historian
Intellectual
Inventor: Innovator, Computer Scientist/Technician
Leader: Negotiator, Debater, Peacemaker
Naturalist: Outdoor Adventurer, Explorer, Leader
Observer: Writer
Scientist
Other Significant Programs/Services

ALTRUIST
Community Servant, Healer, Teacher

Some children want to serve their communities. These community service traits are often identifiable at an early age. They are the healers, the middle school kids who volunteer at the hospital; or they are the teachers, the high school kids who tutor elementary school children in their spare time; they are the kids who want to help the world in some way.

A variety of programs tap into these special altruistic qualities, programs that validate these children's capabilities and give them the confidence and power to contribute and give back to their communities. This section contains programs that serve the community, the country, the world, and the environment.

If a teenager is interested in working in community service, then the Sidwell Friends' Community Service Programs may be the right choice for this child. *Landmark Volunteers* is an exceptional program in which a child can work to preserve America's landmarks; it also provides a youth with insight into the history that surrounds that landmark.

GLOBAL WORKS
Eric Werner, Director
1113 South Allen Street
State College, PA 16801
(814) 867-7000
info@globalworksinc.com
www.globalworksinc.com

QUICK TAKE: A program in which your child can combine community service, the exploration of the world and other cultures, and camping. Children will get to feel the essence of community at the same time as they help people and are introduced to a new and exciting culture. Staff leaders come from all walks of life and have extraordinary résumés.

AGE REQUIREMENT: 15–18 (except programs in New Zealand and Fiji, 14–18)

FEES: Vary by location. The programs usually run between two and four weeks in the summer.

BACKGROUND: Founded in 1988, these programs are located in a variety of locations, including Costa Rica, France, Ecuador, Puerto Rico, Ireland, Spain, Italy, Bolivia/Peru, Fiji Islands/New Zealand, and Yucatan/Mexico. Quebec and the Pacific Northwest are all geared to providing students with a first-hand look at the life and culture of another country.

DESCRIPTION: The kids either live in a home with a family or in facilities within a community. They work on community service projects to help people of the country. As the kids help to restore and build communities, they also make new friends and get to travel and learn the culture of the area. The kids are given time to explore and participate in activities appropriate to the location. Some offer snorkeling and swimming, while others have hiking and kayaking.

OUR TAKE: This is a wonderful experience for any teenager! Your child has the chance to see a completely different world through the eyes of the family with whom he or she is staying and to learn the language and culture of the country. The program offers high school credit, which is always impressive on your kid's high school transcript. But what I find most impressive are the values of the program. Kids will learn to understand that these people lead quality lives with limited material possessions. The program provides perspective, camaraderie, and an experience that will stay with children throughout their lives.

OUR RECOMMENDATION: If your kid has an interest in helping the community and an interest in the environment, have them take a look at the Web site to see if any location interests them. Transportation is provided from local airports.

LANDMARK VOLUNTEERS
Volunteer camp
Ann Barrett, Director
P.O. Box 455
Sheffield, MA 01257
(413) 229-0255
landmark@volunteers.com
www.volunteers.com

QUICK TAKE: A program focused on the joy of community service, offering opportunities for work to preserve our country's national landmarks. Kids leave this program having put in an incredible number of community service hours, yet having had fun at the same time. A typical program might include working on the Cumberland Trail in Tennessee.

AGE REQUIREMENT: 15 and older

FEES: Boarding program, $735. A $50 fee is incurred if application is not received before April 1. Financial aid is based on need and merit.

BACKGROUND: In 1990, a group of educators and community leaders founded Landmark Volunteers to encourage community service. The program has locations in almost every state. Its purpose is to maintain and improve our country's national landmark sites. Work could include anything from making the site handicapped accessible to actually working on the site.

DESCRIPTION: The nationwide program offers two sessions, each lasting two weeks, in June, July, or August. Students engage in service for six days the first week and five days the second. In total, they earn eighty hours of community service! The kids are organized into teams of 13 under the supervision of one adult volunteer. The teams have myriad service jobs to accomplish, ranging from trail building to taking inventory of species. The schedule varies in each camp, but all offer recreational activities in addition to the work.

OUR TAKE: The Landmark Volunteers mean business when it comes to community service, and they expect the most out of students. This is a great opportunity for students who need to complete community service hours for high school credit. The small teams are a great place for your student to meet and make friends as well. Kids leave the program with a feeling of accomplishment. The team experience alone will be an excellent opportunity for your kid to find great friends.

OUR RECOMMENDATION: Landmark Volunteers is one of the best kept secrets around. It will build character, inner strength, and maturity. Students traveling to the camp by public transportation will be met by a counselor.

SIDWELL FRIEND'S COMMUNITY SERVICE PROGRAMS

Janet Carter, Director
3825 Wisconsin Avenue NW
Washington, DC 20016
(202) 537-8133
Fax: (202)537-2483
sidwellsummer@yahoo.com
www.sidwell.edu/summer/summercommunityservice

QUICK TAKE: Sidwell Friend's Community Service Programs present many stimulating community service opportunities, ranging from elder care to environmental clean up to language exchange with different cultures. Through a number of workshops, Sidwell Friend's School offers something for every child and an ideal, positive way for your child to spend his or her summer.

AGE REQUIREMENT: Camp Lend-a-Hand at Riverview (grades 5–10); Costa Rica (ages 13–18); Hawaii (ages 13–18); Spanish Service (grades 9–12); ASL (American Sign Language), Helping Hands, Clean Up!, A, B, C's of Community Service with Infants/Toddlers (grades 5–8); Little Hands, Big Hearts (grades 2–5).

FEES: Call for information.

SPONSORSHIP/OWNERSHIP/ACCREDITATION: Sidwell Friend's School

BACKGROUND: Sidwell Friend's Community Service Programs workshops have been going on for varying durations.

DESCRIPTION: All workshops occur during the summer months. Every workshop includes various components and experiences. Below is a brief overview of each.

Overnight Community Service Workshops

Camp Lend-A-Hand at Riverview: A week-long camp that combines service opportunities with traditional camp experiences. Campers participate in daily projects that include working with different types of service organizations, assisting the elderly, helping local not-for-profit organizations, and cleaning up parks, hiking trails, and other public spaces. One day during the week, the campers will take a break from community service projects to join in an outdoor activity, such as rafting or a ropes course. This camp is held at St. Margaret's School. Transportation is provided from Sidwell Friend's School to St. Margaret's.

Costa Rica: Participants will have the opportunity to explore the rich culture of Costa Rica, to learn and use Spanish, and participate in outdoor activities, such as waterfall swimming, rafting, boating, and horseback riding. Participants also complete five days of service projects that might include such activities as building a community center, working at a school, or teaching local children.

Hawaii: This workshop fosters learning about activities to save Hawaii's native plants and animals. Participants contribute toward conservation and preservation efforts. Most of their time is spent in two wildlife sanctuaries: Koke'e State Park on the island of Kauai and Hakalau National Wildlife Refuge in the mountain forests of the island of Hawaii. In both of these sanctuaries, participants help staff eliminate alien vegetation and re-establish native plants. Participants receive a letter from Sidwell Friend's describing their community service to their schools.

Workshops for High School

Spanish Service: Students in this workshop have the opportunity to improve their Spanish language skills. They work on their pronunciation in a "language laboratory" and participate in dialogs and role plays, write compositions, and give oral reports. Students also have the opportunity to work in service organizations in the Latino community of Washington, DC.

Workshops for Middle School

ASL (American Sign Language): This workshop provides the opportunity to learn and explore the third most common language in the United States. Students will learn how to communicate using signs, facial expressions, and gestures the way most people who are deaf and hard-of-hearing do. Deaf Culture and its many aspects will also be discussed and examined. A field trip to a school for the deaf or a similar site will allow students to practice what they have learned.

Helping Hands: A one-week, full-day workshop that provides hands-on community service opportunities and time for classroom learning and group reflection. During the week, students volunteer at various not-for-profit organizations, such as nursing homes, day care centers, homeless services providers, or environmental agencies. The morning begins in a Sidwell classroom discussing issues important to the service project of the day.

Clear Up!: This workshop engages participants in such activities as cleaning up local parks, beaches, and bays. Participants learn about the environment and their relationship to it in class, through visits to local farms, and by taking canoe trips to view local ecosystems and the systems' impact on native wildlife.

A, B, Cs of Community Service with Infants/Toddlers: In this two-week workshop, participants intern in local daycare centers, spending four hours daily working with infants and children up to age five and their caregivers. They develop activities and assist with a variety of classroom functions. They explore interactions, situations encountered, and learning about early childhood development.

Workshops for Elementary School

Little Hands, Big Hearts: A part of the Explorer Day Camp, this afternoon workshop introduces children to community service. Activities may include art projects for the elderly, a visit to a daycare center to perform a skit, making sandwiches for a shelter, cleaning up a park, and creating stories about how people can help others.

OUR TAKE: With such a wide variety of programs and experiences, a child of any age will benefit greatly from the opportunity to participate in any one of these workshops. This is a great way for your child to gain a healthy sense of altruism, contribute positively and fruitfully to the community, meet new friends, and feel good about himself or herself as an individual. These workshops provide unlimited resources and opportunities for personal growth and heighten your child's levels of community, cultural, environmental, and social awareness.

OUR RECOMMENDATION: The program has more than enough activities for any kid to have a good time. This is a great way for your student to show his or her involvement in the community.

VOLUNTEERS FOR PEACE INTERNATIONAL WORK CAMP
International community service camp
Amy Bannon, Outgoing Placement *or* Peter Coldwell, Director
1034 Tiffany Road
Belmont, VT 05730
(802) 259-2759
vfp@vfp.org
www.vfp.org

QUICK TAKE: This program is definitely for the independent mature kid. The decision to participate must be driven by the teenager. The child must travel to the work camp destination by himself or herself, where he or she will meet and work with other teens who speak different languages. Usually there are only a few English-speaking teens in a group. You have to be a certain type of kid to love this journey. It's hard work. The kids will travel to interesting countries, meet the people, learn about the culture, and engage in community service.

AGE REQUIREMENT: 15 and older for most programs; a few programs each year for 14-year olds.

FEES: Vary with location and length of session: airfare plus $250 registration fee. Check out the Web site for more information on the various camps and prices.

SPONSORSHIP/OWNERSHIP/ACCREDITATION: Volunteers for Peace

BACKGROUND: Since 1982, Volunteers for Peace has been a not-for-profit organization whose purpose is to connect students in countries around the world. The camp's goal is to promote peace and understanding through more interaction among people of different ethnic backgrounds and cultures.

DESCRIPTION: Kids have the opportunity to choose from a number of great locations around the world. Each location offers different workshops and interesting projects. There will also be time to visit with people native to the country and make new friends. Students will also get the chance to learn about the culture and pick up a little of the language. Students have the option of earning college credit through this program.

OUR TAKE: Independent travel is required, and the child must be willing to put up with language barriers. Usually programs go Germany and France, but some are in Estonia and Italy. If your child is on the way to the Peace Corps, let him or her have a look at this camp. This is a great way for students to study abroad and learn about different cultures as they help a community and have a great time. College credit is an added bonus.

OUR RECOMMENDATION: The decision to go on this type of trip must be made by the child. NOTE: Parents who are Peace Corps *wannabes*—don't live vicariously through your child. It takes a mature, independent, and energetic kid to make this summer work. These qualities are essential to a successful summer for your child. They have an immense amount of credentials and opportunities for the volunteer student. This program gives students the opportunity to explore a new place and feel the joy and rewards of volunteer work. Its goal is to help kids learn more about other countries, along with a camp experience that they'll never forget!

ARTIST
Musician, Performer

B ringing out the artist in a child can only be enriching. Whether your child has artistic talent worthy of a "professional-in-training"; simply enjoys singing, dancing, and/or performing for the fun of it; or just loves the camaraderie that comes from an artistic endeavor, there is a program in this category to evaluate.

There are worlds of possibilities available to the artistic child. French Woods Festival of the Performing Arts is one of options for the child who wants to try out life on the stage. For the teen who is a budding Steven Spielberg, a devotee of film, and a prefocused director in the making; then the New York Film Academy is the pre-eminent school involved in teaching kids the art of moviemaking. And for those West Coast film buffs, the New York Film Academy has a Los Angeles program.

For the child who wants a summer camp and artistic experience at the same time, there is Hidden Valley Camp, which is a traditional summer camp for that artistically inclined and interested child.

The name Juilliard connotes quality in music and performance. For the child who dreams of becoming a dancer, this is an opportunity of a lifetime. Children can experience a program of the highest caliber, and, through this experience, can decide if this is a dream that they truly want to pursue. Those of you on the West Coast may want to consider one of the many different arts programs offered by the California State School for the Arts.

CALIFORNIA STATE SUMMER SCHOOL FOR THE ARTS CAMP

Cynthia Bextine, Office Technician
1010 Hurley Way, Suite 185
Sacramento, CA 95819
(916) 227-9320
cynthia@csssa.org
www.csssa.org

QUICK TAKE: An art camp for students really focused on one of the many art forms performed here. From dance to visual arts, this camp will strengthen your student's skills. The camp's purpose is to give every student enough training to pursue art as a future profession.

AGE REQUIREMENT: 14–18

FEES: Application fee, $20; boarding program, $1,590–$3,800 Financial aid is available.

SPONSORSHIP/OWNERSHIP/ACCREDITATION: California State University

BACKGROUND: In 1987, the California legislature began this school for individuals who have a strong leaning toward visual, cinematic, music, or performing arts. It is held at the California Institute of the Arts, whose goal is to encourage kids in their field of interest and to provide a promising future for them in their careers.

DESCRIPTION: The camp offers an intensive four-week session in July in seven departments (animation, creative writing, dance, film and video, music, theater, and the visual arts) and gives three credits from California State University to those who successfully complete the course. Each program has a set work schedule (from 8 AM to 4 PM) and afterwards students can rehearse or give informal performances of their work. Recreational activities are offered on the weekends, and there are some optional field trips to places such as Six Flags and the Getty Museum. Transportation is available from the Hollywood/Burbank Airport on the first and last days; reservations are required.

OUR TAKE: This is a really useful program for the ambitious art student. Many opportunities are opened to a student after spending only four weeks at this camp. It would be beneficial for any art student.

OUR RECOMMENDATION: The program requires a lot of time and energy on your child's part. Students are accepted based on their talent and creativity, so it's pretty competitive. Before applying, make sure your kid knows the set-up of this camp and is willing to devote a large amount of time to his or her art.

FRENCH WOODS FESTIVAL OF THE PERFORMING ARTS

Summer:
P.O. Box 009
Hancock, NY 13783
Winter:
P.O. Box 770100
Coral Springs, FL 33077-0100
admin@frenchwoods.com
www.frenchwoods.com

QUICK TAKE: Located in New York's beautiful western Catskills just over 100 miles from New York City, this festival invites kids from around the country and world interested in performing to "participate in a program run by certified teachers and complemented by counselor specialists." With campers coming from New York, Philadelphia, Florida, and even London or Paris, meeting a diverse group of kids is a plus.

AGE REQUIREMENT: 7–17

FEES: One week precamp, $650; first three weeks of summer, $3,400; second three weeks of summer, $3,900; last three weeks of summer, $2,850; first six weeks, $6,200; last six weeks, $5,000; full nine weeks, $7,000. Fees include a nonrefundable $350 instruction, supervision, and room and board fee.

BACKGROUND: French Woods Festival of the Performing Arts, which started in 1970, now includes dance, theater, music, circus, magic, visual arts, and sports. Begun as a quiet camp, it has become the preeminent program for kids interested in performing arts, nontraditional sports, and everything in between.

DESCRIPTION: From the Web site: "Each day consists of six activity periods, three majors and three minors. Majors are chosen at the beginning of each session, meet daily and are activities you have the most interest in pursuing. Majors are instructional and are designed to meet your individual ability level. At French Woods, many majors lead towards a Festival Week performance. Minors are chosen daily to explore new interests. If you prefer, you can strengthen the areas of strong interest during the minor periods." Most activities involve eight to twelve children. The campers are grouped and bunked together by age. An out-of-camp trip to New York City is available for the foreign (both to the country and area) campers, and sometimes children will leave camp "to compete in intercamp games or perform in our traveling troupes."

OUR TAKE: Kids love the idea of being able to make their own decisions. At French Woods, they get to choose their activities, and they're never stopped from doing what they choose.

Furthermore, the staff is skilled in motivation, problem solving, and just letting kids have fun.

OUR RECOMMENDATION: When we hear "performing arts," we think of the relatively narrow areas of theater, dance, and music. But French Woods offers much more: it offers a new way to behave, play, and learn.

HIDDEN VALLEY CAMP
Creative and performing arts camp
Peter & Meg Kassen, Directors/Owners
161 Hidden Valley Road
Freedom, ME 04941
(207) 342-5177
summer@hiddenvalleycamp.com
www.hiddenvalleycamp.com

QUICK TAKE: This is not a traditional or average camp. Rather, it is a noncompetitive camp immersed strongly in the arts. The directors do it well. It's choice driven for the kid who is independent and works well in a less-structured environment. Hidden Valley Camp welcomes students from across the country and around the world for arts and crafts, horseback riding, music, sports, swimming—you name it. Children can also participate in day trips and special performing arts events. The camp stresses building self-esteem. A camp newspaper, sign language, and organic farming are elements that make this experience exceptional.

AGE REQUIREMENT: 8–13.

FEES: Four-week camp, $3,690; eight weeks, $5,990. (Most kids attend for only four weeks.) Some activities, such as horseback riding, require an additional fee, but most activities are included in the tuition.

BACKGROUND: Hidden Valley Camp began in 1948 "as a work and farm camp for twelve teenaged campers." Since then, the still family-owned business (now by Peter and Meg Kassen) has evolved into one of the best-known camps in the country for the child who wants a noncompetitive camp strongly committed to the arts and emphasizing the personal discovery of self through a diverse and eclectic program.

DESCRIPTION: The kids are free to choose which classes (arts and crafts, waterfront swimming, riding, ropes courses, performing arts, sports, outdoor adventures, music, llama and animal care, communication arts (which includes video, photography, journalism, and creative writing)) to take from those offered during one-hour instruction periods. For four to eight weeks (depending on your choice), your child will be placed in an atmosphere that emphasizes his or her chosen activities. As with most camps, there are the traditional out-of-camp day trips to roller skating rinks, the circus, and so on. The camp is committed to enhancing self-esteem through its well-trained staff and exceptional programs.

OUR TAKE: This camp is for the open-minded thinker. It is for the independent child who would enjoy exploring himself or herself through a strong creative program. If your child is a competitive sports enthusiast, this may not be the program. For those parents, who want to broaden the horizons of their athletically driven kid, this may be the answer. One caveat: If your child operates best and thrives in a structured environment, this is not the optimal choice.

OUR RECOMMENDATION: A summer at Hidden Valley might give children the confidence to learn what they are good at.

JUILLIARD SUMMER DANCE INTENSIVE PROGRAM
Performance camp
Andra Corvino, Director
The Juilliard School Admissions Office
60 Lincoln Center Plaza,
New York, NY 10023-6588
(212) 799-5000 ext. 270
summerdance@juilliard.edu
www.juilliard.edu/summer/dance.html

QUICK TAKE: An intensive summer dance program for any child who has been dreaming of becoming a dancer. This camp focuses especially on dance to give the student the feel of how challenging and rewarding the art can be.

AGE REQUIREMENT: 15–17

FEES: Application fee, $35; tuition, $825; room and board, $825. Financial aid is available.

SPONSORSHIP/OWNERSHIP/ACCREDITATION: The Juilliard School

BACKGROUND: The Juilliard School is known for nurturing dancers, musicians, and performers. The Summer Dance Intensive Program was founded about six years ago to give high school students a taste of the devotion and drive needed to succeed at this excellent institution and in the performing arts.

DESCRIPTION: During the three-week session from July into August, students begin their day focusing on technique under professional faculty as they work in the studio on ballet technique, *pointe work*, and partnering. In the afternoon, the students attend a modern dance class and work on ballroom dance. Their evenings are taken up with rehearsing new dances that will be performed at the end of the program. Although the days are full of intensive practice, there is still time on some evenings and weekends to explore the theatre of Broadway and New York City. An audition tape is required.

OUR TAKE: This is an intensive program designed for kids who have reached an advanced level. Acceptance in this program is very selective. If your student has devoted an incredible amount of time and energy to dance, then this camp may be the ticket to getting his or her foot in the door when applying for college.

OUR RECOMMENDATION: Make sure that your child has the determination and drive to work as intensely as this program requires. If he or she does, it will be an exciting and enriching experience.

NEW YORK FILM ACADEMY (NYFA)
Moving Art
David Klein, Senior Director
100 East 17 Street
New York, NY 10003
(212) 674-4300
www.nyfa.com

QUICK TAKE: Whether a student's background is in film or not, this institution, the self-dubbed "hands-on film school," will give young adults a solid film background—in front of or behind the camera.

AGE REQUIREMENT: 14 and older

FEES: From $5,900 for the 4-week filmmaking course to $6,900 for the 6-week course. This does not include room and board.

BACKGROUND: The New York Film Academy was established in 1993 "on a belief that a top quality education in filmmaking should be accessible to anyone with the drive and ambition to make films." Kids' programs are held only in the summer. Entertainment industry icons Steven Spielberg and Pierce Brosnan, among others, have sent their sons to the New York Film Academy.

DESCRIPTION: Courses vary in subject and length.

AMC (American Movie Classics): A one-week program held in conjunction with American Movie Channel, this is a crash course in filmmaking for students who have no experience. There are no expectations, and it teaches the basics.

4-Week and 6-Week Filmmaking Workshop: The four-week course teaches your child all the basics of how to work with a 16-mm camera. The six-week program offers greater depth.

5-Week Digital Program: This course teaches your child the basics of digital filmmaking.

4-Week Acting Program: This program teaches the basics of acting. Some kids may have some experience, but many don't.

The curriculum offers intense training. Directing, camera operation, editing, filmmaking, and acting programs are available. Individuals with little to no filmmaking experience are asked to take advantage of the Total Immersion Workshop, which gives students a crash course in every aspect of filmmaking. The Academy's Web site says the intensity of its courses demands maturity, commitment, dedication, and the ability to work with others.

Multilocation School: New York, Los Angeles, London, Harvard University in Cambridge, Massachusetts, and Princeton University in New Jersey. Some higher education institutions offer college credit for courses taken at the New York Film Academy.

HOUSING

New York/Dalton Program: There is no formal housing provided for high-school age students for the New York City/Dalton program. If it is a New York venue to which your child is committed, contact Anita Gan and she will assist your child on an individual basis. Remember, there is no after-hours supervision, so it may be wise to accompany your child or have a friend or relative nearby for supervision.

Universal Studios/Los Angeles Program: Housing is at the Oakwood Apartments. It is not a campus dorm. Two- and four-person accommodations are available.

London Kings College Campus: Housing is not on this campus, but at a nearby college campus which is within walking distance of the school.

Harvard/Princeton University Campuses: Housing is on campus. If you want a more campus-oriented support situation, this is where your child should go.

OUR TAKE: In filmmaking, people who "think outside the box" are the norm, not the exception, and they are usually the ones who become successful. The NYFA is an institution that has become successful largely because of its outside-the-box thinking. For the kid who isn't a big fan of formal schooling, but is interested in getting an education in something he or she loves, the New York Film Academy is something to look into. A summer at the NYFA looks positive on a résumé. An education from the NYFA, with its long work days and hands-on training, can prepare a child for all the world has to offer.

OUR RECOMMENDATION: If your child is serious about the movie business, this is a strong program and the place to be. The staff is serious and from "the business." There are potential advantages and drawbacks inherent to each venue. The NYFA staff will work with you. Do your research. It's really up to you.

PRINCETON BALLET SCHOOL JUNIOR, SENIOR, AND INTENSIVE PROGRAMS
Ballet camp
Mary Robertson, Director
301 North Harrison Street
Princeton, NJ 08540
(609) 921-7758
www.arballet.org

QUICK TAKE: A camp that is focused on the art of dance and transforming students into professionals. There are three camps in which students can begin at an early age and develop the technique and skills to achieve grace and agility. This dance program is unmatched.

ACE REQUIREMENT: Junior program, 9–13; senior program, 11–14; intensive program, 13–20.

FEES: Application fee, $20. Each program offers a different number of sessions; therefore, the prices vary: Junior Day Program, $460 to $985; Senior Day Program, $495 to $1,155. The Intensive Day Program, $1,350 and Boarding Program, $3,000. Financial aid is available.

SPONSORSHIP/OWNERSHIP/ACCREDITATION: Princeton University

BACKGROUND: The Princeton Ballet School (The name changed to the American Repertory Ballet in 1991) was founded in 1954 by Audreé Estey and has been graduating professional dancers ever since. The Ballet School Summer program began in 1999 to help aspiring young dancers practice their form and understand the skill and endurance needed to become a professional dancer.

DESCRIPTION: There is an intensive schedule for each program. The Junior group focuses on improving the students' flexibility and strength, along with their form. The class studies a few forms of dance, such as folk and modern. The Seniors also work on ballet technique, but jazz, modern, and other forms of dance are incorporated into the schedule. The Intensive program teaches how to dance and prevent injury, as well as creative choreography.

OUR TAKE: Becoming a dancer takes an enormous amount of time, and it is best to begin at a very young age. All three of these programs are key to helping aspiring dancers improve their technique and to helping them understand the pressure and pain it takes to become an excellent dancer. These programs will help your kid on the path to becoming a professional dancer.

OUR RECOMMENDATION: If your child is eligible, contact the Director for more information. This is a once in a lifetime experience for a dancer!

SUMMER THEATRE INSTITUTE
Performing arts camp
Allyn Sitjar, Director
Summer Theatre Institute
Youth Theatre of New Jersey
23 Tomahawk Trail
Sparta, NJ 07871
(201) 415-5329
youththeatreallyn@yahoo.com

QUICK TAKE: This is a theater camp like no other program available. The Summer Theatre Institute is based in New York City amid the great shows of Broadway. Here, students will get the opportunity to work with professional instructors and learn about various aspects of the theater. A great program for any student wishing to apply to a college-level theater program.

AGE REQUIREMENT: 14–19

SPONSORSHIP/OWNERSHIP/ACCREDITATION: Columbia University

FEES: Application fee, $55. Room and board, $4,600 to $4,800 (early enrollment discount may apply).

BACKGROUND: The Youth Theatre of New Jersey is an intense theater program for young aspiring actors. In 1989, the Youth Theatre began a program called the Summer Theatre Institute at Columbia University in New York City. The main goal of the camp is to create a healthy, respectful environment for kids to explore various acting skills.

DESCRIPTION: The Summer Institute is a professional camp for kids to try their hand at one of many aspects of theater. All students will be in core classes, which will help with acting, improvisation, and speech. Students may concentrate on one of these four categories: Actors, Musical Theater Actors, Playwrights, and Directors. In each group, students will work with professionals and be encouraged to create new forms of theater. Each session is about four weeks in either June or July.

OUR TAKE: This is definitely a theater camp for the best of the best. Columbia is an Ivy League college, and students will get first-hand experience in going to school in a busy city. With programs for every student's interest, attendees will gain a great deal from this experience.

OUR RECOMMENDATION: This is a very focused camp, so make sure your kid is really interested.

ATHLETE
Competitor

The United States has hundreds of sports programs and camps to meet your child's needs. Your choice will depend on whether your child is looking for a competitive program or one that is less intent on "the win," more relaxed, and more interested in teaching the sport, playing the game, and having fun.

This section reviews the U.S.A. Slider Search, which is the name for the U.S. Olympic Luge Team Recruitment Effort. This is one example of how a parent may involve a child in an Olympic Sport. There are many other Olympic sports, and some are more competitive than others and some offer greater opportunity for involvement.

OLYMPIC REGIONAL DEVELOPMENT AUTHORITY
Olympic sports camp
Brad Clark, Director
Lake Placid, NY 12946
(518) 523-1655 ext. 250
bclark@orda.org
www.orda.org

QUICK TAKE: Do you ever wonder how kids make it to the Olympic Winter Games? Well it's obvious that they choose a sport, work hard, and dedicate their lives to it. ORDA is a good place to begin. If your child has an affinity for the bobsled, ORDA is where he or she must train. It's a camp where students get to "be" the people in the bobsled and "be" the people skiing. This program provides the knowledge and training needed to start working on Olympic sports. The program also includes opportunities to see the area and the Winter Olympic Museum.

AGE REQUIREMENT: The earlier the better—grade school age and older.

FEES: One-day rate for the day camp, $65; multiday rates available. Training and classes take place at ORDA.

BACKGROUND: Lake Placid Gold Medal Games encourage teamwork and camaraderie through group sports. Classes are held in the summer and winter; sports offered vary with the season. The Gold Medal Adventure Day Camp is held from June to September.

DESCRIPTION: This is where a child can get that Winter Olympics feel. However, if the Summer Olympics is your kid's thing, you can also begin your research here. The Gold Medal Adventure Day Camp provides the equipment needed to participate in the many sports it offers, among them the luge, freestyle skiing, canoeing, and bobsledding. Before the students start practicing, they will be trained under professionals to ensure safety. Students will also receive lunch and are given the chance to tour the 1932 and 1980 Olympic Winter Museum.

OUR TAKE: This is the best way for your child to understand firsthand what it takes to be an Olympic athlete. This is a great way for students to learn to work together and make new friends as they learn and play amazing sports. The camp allows for many adventures during the day, plus time to see the awe-inspiring memorabilia in the museum. There are so many programs available to all ages that this could be a fun-filled family vacation. See the Web site for more information.

OUR RECOMMENDATION: The camp is designed to allow time for leisure and for beginners to learn to ski/bobsled/luge or participate in any other sport and could really get your child thinking about the devotion and time it takes to become an Olympian.

U.S.A. SLIDER SEARCH
U.S. Olympic Luge Team Recruitment Effort
Registration Department
35 Church Street
Lake Placid, NY 12946-1805
(800) USA-LUGE
info@usaluge.org
www.usaluge.org/slidersearch

QUICK TAKE: Step one in the recruitment effort of the highly decorated U.S. Olympic Luge Team. If your child is an Olympic hopeful looking for a sport that has an on-going recruitment effort, then the USA Slider Search is for your child. Even for the kids who don't qualify for the intensive one-week winter training camp in Lake Placid, New York, this program offers fun and challenges.

AGE REQUIREMENT: 10–14

FEE: Registration, $15.

SPONSORSHIP/OWNERSHIP/ACCREDITATION: Verizon USA

BACKGROUND: This program was established in 1986 by Bonnie Warner, a former luge athlete from California. Today, the Slider Search conducts annual searches in eight cities across the United States and is the primary source for finding talent for the U.S. Luge team. Aspiring athletes are offered the opportunity to participate in the weekend programs, designed to recruit kids for the team.

DESCRIPTION: Throughout the summer, the Slider Search team travels to different quadrants of the country for weekend sessions in which kids learn the nuances of competing in the luge. They are shown actual equipment used in the Winter Games and are introduced to the summer equipment, which is a sled anchored by inline skating wheels. Then, the kids are taken to a slope where they gradually go further distances and are presented with increasingly difficult obstacles. Finally, a small battery of fitness tests and an obstacle course are given to test the kids' athletic abilities. Strong upper-body strength is a plus. At the end of the summer, the most promising 75 from the more than 800 participants come to Lake Placid in the winter for one of three one-week training camps (25 kids per camp).

OUR TAKE: What we really like about the U.S.A. Luge Slider Search is that everyone gets to participate. Even if the kid isn't gifted enough to make it to Lake Placid in the winter, he or she gets a chance to have fun, learn a new sport, and get a feel for the competitive process. The bottom line is that for a very nominal expenditure a child can try out for the Olympics and possibly make it to the next step. It's an experience and an event from which memories are made.

OUR RECOMMENDATION: If you plan ahead your child can prepare a bit, improve upper body strength, and possibly even practice on a summer luge to get a feel for the sport. It's an accessible opportunity for a child to fulfill his/her dream and focus on a competitive objective. Who knows, the next step could be the Lake Placid luge track.

DESIGNER
Architect

When children decide on a profession, they usually feel that only a limited number of options are available: they can be a teacher, doctor, lawyer, police officer, firefighter, president, or mayor. Yet, how many times have you looked at the cover of your child's notebook and seen doodles that are so sophisticated and designs so advanced that you feel your kid has the makings of an architect, fashion designer, or interior designer? The programs offered in this section provide a perfect opportunity to expose your child to careers in design.

The Fashion Institute of Technology (FIT), located in the "fashion capital of the world," New York City, offers teens who design their own "different" fashions the opportunity to turn these ideas into a fashion trend at its summer program. For your jewelry maker, take a look at the Rhode Island School of Design program. Catholic University in Washington, DC, and Washington University in St. Louis, both offer programs in architecture.

These programs expose teens to areas that might otherwise go unacknowledged. The talent of these children is often unappreciated until they enter their desired professions. These programs offer them the opportunity for earlier recognition and may help to build their self-esteem.

CATHOLIC UNIVERSITY EXPERIENCES IN ARCHITECTURE
Architecture camp
Jeff Roberson, Director
Catholic University
620 Michigan Avenue NE
Washington, DC 20064
(202) 319-5188
loosle@cua.edu
www.summer.cua.edu

QUICK TAKE: This intensive study of architecture allows young adults to explore the magnificent architecture of Washington, DC and gives them a backstage pass to architects' offices, as well as trips to construction sites. Students also gain the experience of living in a college dorm. The university offers various sports from swimming to racquetball.

AGE REQUIREMENT: 15–18

FEES: Day program, $915–$1,025. Room and board, $1,200. Financial aid is available.

SPONSORSHIP/OWNERSHIP/ACCREDITATION: Catholic University of America

BACKGROUND: The Catholic University of America was founded in 1887 by Catholic bishops whose goal was to establish a university that challenges the student's intellect. The university has a wide range of colleges and majors to accommodate the student's focus and offers many summer programs to suit any young adult's interests.

DESCRIPTION: The program consists of two three-week sessions in June and July. Campers analyze and observe many of DC's famous buildings and monuments. The students also visit local architects and nearby construction sites.

OUR TAKE: If your son or daughter has a deep interest in a specific field, this program will help him or her gain a greater understanding of the subject and will be a plus on college applications, especially if an architecture school is in the future.

OUR RECOMMENDATION: The camp is very focused, so make sure your son or daughter is willing to devote the summer to intense, but enjoyable, study.

FASHION INSTITUTE OF TECHNOLOGY: SUMMER LIVE AT FIT

Fashion design camp
Center for Pre-College Programs
Seventh Avenue at 27 Street
New York, NY 10001
(212) 217-7882
www.fitnyc.edu

QUICK TAKE: Kids are in control as they express their creative side and study at an institute that recruits students who definitely think outside the box. At FIT, students are given the chance to attend classes and experience courses in fashion, computer technology, and other related subjects.

AGE REQUIREMENT: 11–18

FEES: New York residents, $250 for one class, $485 for two; out-of-state, $325 for one class, $635 for two classes. No boarding program is available, but contact the program director for information about housing in the area.

SPONSORSHIP/OWNERSHIP/ACCREDITATION: Fashion Institute of Technology

BACKGROUND: Started in 1944 as a small school, FIT has become a leading venue for the study of fashion. It also offers programs in design, computer technology, merchandising, production, and more.

DESCRIPTION: The program, which runs for three weeks in July, allows students to take one or two classes from FIT's popular fashion courses, as well as classes in advertising, marketing, and jewelry design. Field trips to many museums and industry showrooms acquaint youngsters with the realities of a career in fashion.

OUR TAKE: This would be a great opportunity for the creative student who wants to learn the fashion ropes and get some useful background in marketing, advertising, and more.

OUR RECOMMENDATION: If your child is interested in fashion design, this is probably the best place to be. It's a great head start! Since there is no boarding program, it is best to check early to see what is available nearby.

PARSONS PRE-COLLEGE ACADEMY
Design camp
Charlotte Rice, Director
Office Pre-enrollment programs
2 West 13 Street
New York, NY 10011
(212) 229-8925
ricec@newschool.edu
www.parsons.edu/ce

QUICK TAKE: An art design camp that allows students to spread their wings and explore any type of art they choose. Students are guided by a talented faculty as they begin to experience the fun of design and evaluate how they can use this tool in college.

AGE REQUIREMENT: 9–18

FEES: Application fee, $7; day program, $168–$672 depending on the length of the program. Financial aid is available.

SPONSORSHIP/OWNERSHIP/ACCREDITATION: Parsons School of Design

BACKGROUND: Originally called the Chase School, the Parsons School was founded by impressionist painter William Merrit Chase in 1896. Frank Alvah Parsons, who joined Chase in 1904 and later became president of the institution, helped to make the school the first institute in fashion and interior design. In 1939, the name was changed. Parsons is a leader in fashion, computer, and architecture design education. The summer program began in 2000 to acquaint aspiring students with the world of professional art design.

DESCRIPTION: The program ranges from five to eleven days every month, except June. The attendees are divided into three groups based on their level of study: Elementary—for rising 4th, 5th, and 6th graders, who attend in the morning; Junior—for 7th, 8th, and 9th graders, and Senior—for 10th, 11th ,and 12th graders, who attend morning and afternoon sessions. All students focus on electives of their choice, which range from animation design to fashion to photography. Junior and senior students must also enroll in Drawing Studio, which is held in the morning.

OUR TAKE: This is an excellent opportunity for a student interested in any of the many types of art design offered at Parsons. The students also receive college credit, which will look great on college applications.

OUR RECOMMENDATION: This is a program for artistically talented kids, and it shouldn't be passed up! Since housing is not provided, if you live outside the New York metropolitan area, you may want to call on friends or relatives or consider a vacation in the city.

PRATT INSTITUTE SUMMER PRE-COLLEGE PROGRAM FOR HIGH SCHOOL STUDENTS
Art and architecture camp
Joelle Danant, Administrator
Center for Continuing and Professional Studies
ISC Building, Room 205
200 Willoughby Avenue
Brooklyn, NY 11205-9975
(718) 636-3453
prostudies@pratt.edu
www.prostudies.pratt.edu

QUICK TAKE: For any high school student who wants to work in design or architecture, this would be an excellent place. This camp is part of the well-known arts school, Pratt. Here your student will work to improve his or her understanding in many fields of art and get to make a portfolio. The student also earns college credit after attending.

AGE REQUIREMENT: 16–18

SPONSORSHIP/OWNERSHIP/ACCREDITATION: Pratt Institute

FEES: Boarding program, $3,000. $1,850 for students who commute. Merit-based financial aid is available.

BACKGROUND: The Pratt Institute was founded in 1887 by Charles Pratt, who wanted to create a college focused on art, design, and architecture. The college has campuses in Brooklyn and Manhattan, both in close proximity to theaters, museums, and galleries. This summer program is available to high school students who desire a future in the arts, and it affords them the opportunity to work on their portfolios and earn college credit.

DESCRIPTION: The Manhattan campus is only for commuter students; Brooklyn accepts residential students and commuters. The students will work within their subject areas, but must also take four required courses: Foundation of Art and Design, Art History Appreciation, Portfolio Development, and one elective. Other classes include Graphic Design, Illustration, Fashion Design (only offered in Brooklyn), Photography, and Painting and Drawing. On weekends there are opportunities to visit New York City and see art exhibits and architecture. The thirty-day session occurs in July.

OUR TAKE: If your student has a strong interest in the arts, Pratt should be on your list. The school has much to offer the aspiring art student, and it has the culture of New York City in its backyard.

OUR RECOMMENDATION: This is an extremely intense program; applicants should be reasonably certain that their future lies in art. Check the Web site and call the administrator for additional information.

RHODE ISLAND SCHOOL OF DESIGN PRE-COLLEGE
Art camp
Marc Torlck, Summer Foundation Program
Division of Continuing Education
2 College Street
Providence, RI 02903
(401) 454-6200
summer@risd.edu
www.risd.edu/summer.cfm

QUICK TAKE: This arts program helps students understand art as a major. It is located at the Rhode Island School of Design, near the town College Hill. The students are given challenging art classes in their own field of choice. The knowledge acquired in this camp will help your student with his or her plans for college.

AGE REQUIREMENT: 16–18

FEES: The day program is between $2,900 and $3,600. The boarding program is from $3,800 to $4,200. Financial aid is available based on need and merit.

SPONSORSHIP/OWNERSHIP/ACCREDITATION: Rhode Island School of Design

BACKGROUND: Since its inception in 1970, the program has been allowing high school students from around the world to experience an intense artistic atmosphere. The program is directed at students who want art as a career and those who are interested in complementing their liberal arts work.

DESCRIPTION: Students select their focus from a variety of programs (from fashion and jewelry design to photography and painting). The students must take three required courses: foundation drawing, basic design, and art history. The schedule is packed with work from 7:30 AM to 11 PM on weekdays, with some of this time devoted to independent out-of-class work. The camp lasts for six weeks during the summer.

OUR TAKE: An excellent program for students with an interest in the arts. It puts students on track when it comes time to prepare their portfolios for college applications.

OUR RECOMMENDATION: This is a very focused and rigorous program, so before sending your kid, make sure he or she understands the background of the camp. It's located in a safe and scenic environment for students and is near other great colleges in the Boston area.

WASHINGTON UNIVERSITY IN ST. LOUIS: ARCHITECTURE DISCOVERY PROGRAM

Architecture Camp
Sandy Brennan, Director
Campus Box 1079
Givens Hall, Room 105
One Brookings Drive
St. Louis, MO 63130
(314) 935-6200
www.wustl.edu/

QUICK TAKE: A camp designed for juniors and seniors who are really interested in a future in architecture. Set in the beautiful city of St. Louis, this camp has a driven and strong faculty whose members allow students the freedom to create projects as they acquaint them with the field. This is a great experience that takes college searching to a new level, where students can receive a better feel for campus life.

AGE REQUIREMENT: 16–18

FEES: Application fee, $30. Boarding Program, $1,200 to $1,500.

SPONSORSHIP/OWNERSHIP/ACCREDITATION. Washington University in St. Louis

BACKGROUND: Washington University was founded in 1853. The Discovery Program began in 1985 with the goal of offering high school students the opportunity to get a real feel for college and the opportunity to explore a potential career choice.

DESCRIPTION: This fifteen-day program takes place each June. Each day is divided into two sessions. In the morning, students attend lectures or seminars, visit construction sites, and more. In the afternoon (and sometimes in the evenings), they work on their projects in the School of Architecture. The Art and Architecture Library next door is also available to them. Students are given time on the weekends to enjoy the architecture of St. Louis and understand its function.

OUR TAKE: Programs that offer students a glimpse into the college atmosphere and provide insight into a potential major are an excellent way to get your student prepared for the college search.

OUR RECOMMENDATION: See if your high school student has a genuine interest in architecture. Sign your child up, if he or she hopes to study in that field. If not, there are several other university summer camps that cover a wide variety of interests.

ENTREPRENEUR
Financier, Economist

Creating a business from an idea is an amazing accomplishment, a combination of air and a little bit of capital; but then that's what an entrepreneur does. An entrepreneur can also be a lemonade stand owner, a paperboy with his own route, a baseball card collector who trades up until he or she has the "perfect" deck, or it can be the junior high school girl who creates a summer day camp for the local kids in her backyard.

Enterprising kids are often overlooked until adulthood. Finding programs that tap into their entrepreneurial spirit will help build resilience and instill self-reliance. These programs start in your own community and are usually implemented in junior high and high school. The Wharton Business School Leadership in Business Program is an example of a program that offers high school seniors the opportunity to attend a camp in which they can explore the field of business and leadership and have fun at the same time.

JULIAN KRINSKY BUSINESS SCHOOL AT WHARTON: LEADERSHIP IN THE BUSINESS WORLD
Leadership camp
Julian Krinsky Business School
610 South Anderson Road
King of Prussia, PA 19406
(800) TRY-JKST
info@jkst.commailto:information@nslcleaders.org
www.jkst.com

QUICK TAKE: A camp where kids can explore their interests in the fields of business and leadership, with time for recreational activities. The Julian Krinsky School offers students the chance to live at Haverford University and take courses in business

AGE REQUIREMENT: Entering high school seniors

FEES: Boarding program, $4,000

DATES: 4 weeks from July to August.

SPONSORSHIP/OWNERSHIP/ACCREDITATION: Wharton School of Business, University of Pennsylvania

BACKGROUND: Julian Krinsky camps are located in several states and provide a variety of programs to suit any kid's interests. This program is held at Haverford College in Philadelphia. The camp is offers a traditional summer camp experience, with exciting activities for kids, along with academic concentration.

DESCRIPTION: "Leadership in the Business World" encompasses all parts of business and helps students to wrap their minds around the many issues of the market. They get to learn about career planning, equity, loans, and advertising, all while still enjoying their summer vacation.

OUR TAKE: This is a great way for your student to become knowledgeable about the business world, but still have some time for "R&R" before high school classes resume and get the experience of living in a college environment.

OUR RECOMMENDATION: If your kid wants to know more about ideas and careers in business, then sign up! Your child will get the fun of a camp, plus knowledge of the business world.

HISTORIAN

History shows that the past can teach us about the present by explaining who we are today and how we got here. The ideal is that the lessons of the past will be applied to present problems to create a more positive future.

The three programs listed in this section provide exciting hands-on programs to spark a child's imagination and provide knowledge and experiences that can shape his or her future.

The Alabama Museum of Natural History Summer Expedition allows kids to participate in an archaeological dig and provides an opportunity to see the process by which history is uncovered.

The American Museum of Natural History offers a strong group of programs that cover a variety of areas.

The Rust College Study Abroad in Africa program enables a group of kids to learn about African history and culture and how it relates to our country. Kids come away with a first-hand view of Africa and an experience that may change their lives.

ALABAMA MUSEUM OF NATURAL HISTORY
SUMMER EXPEDITION
ARCHEOLOGY CAMP
Judy Hamilton
Box 870340
Tuscaloosa, AL 35487
(205) 348-0534
Museum.expedition@ua.edu

QUICK TAKE: A camp for future archeologists and paleontologists. Kids get the chance to do extensive research at a natural history museum to experience college living, and receive credit. What's unique is that a parent may also attend.

AGE REQUIREMENT: 14 and older.

FEES: The boarding program is between $350 and $400. Financial aid is available.

DATES: Four six-day sessions in June and July

SPONSORSHIP/OWNERSHIP/ACCREDITATION: Alabama Museum of Natural History, University of Alabama

BACKGROUND: Begun 1979, the program provides students with opportunities for research and gives them a greater understanding of the natural sciences.

DESCRIPTION: Students stay at the University of Alabama, attend such courses as archaeology, botany, and geology; and get some hands-on experience in archaeology and paleontology. There are also opportunities for field research and other expeditions. High school and college credit can be earned on successful completion of the program.

OUR TAKE: This program will give your child insight into how discoveries are made by the people at the Museum of Natural History through the research and study of artifacts. It's a great way to meet new friends with similar interests, and the college credit will look impressive on your child's transcript.

OUR RECOMMENDATION: This expedition will provide your child with the feel of an archeological "dig." It's a great place to begin, if your kid is interested in archeology.

AMERICAN MUSEUM OF NATURAL HISTORY CAMP
American Museum of Natural History
Central Park West at 79 Street
New York, NY 10024-5192
(212) 769-5758
www.amnh.org/programs/summer

QUICK TAKE: Take a walk on the surface of Mars, trace the evolution of homo sapiens' cousin, learn the difference in diet between a seal and a manatee, use Legos™ to construct your very own Mars explorer. These programs held at one of the world's finest museums will excite and stimulate your child.

AGE REQUIREMENT: Destination Space: Astrophysics 1 (Minisession), Astrophysics 2 (incoming 2nd–3rd graders) Astrophysics 3 (incoming 4th–5th graders); Positively Primates: Primatology (Minisession) (incoming 4th–5th graders); Robotics 1 (incoming 6th–7th graders), Robotics 2 (4th–5th graders); Oceans to Ocean Life 1 (incoming 4th–5th graders) Oceans to Ocean Life 2 (incoming 2nd–3rd graders); Frogs 1 (incoming 4th–5th graders), Frogs 2 (incoming 2nd–3rd graders).

FEES: Average fee for a 5-day program is $350.

SPONSORSHIP/OWNERSHIP/ACCREDITATION: American Museum of Natural History

BACKGROUND: Programs range from 2 to 5 days and have been offered by the American Museum of Natural History for many years.

DESCRIPTION: Below is a brief description of each of the AMNH Adventures programs available in 2005. Every program includes hands-on investigations, behind-the-scenes tours, and visits with museum scientists.

Destination Space: Astrophysics I: Students explore what it would be like to live, work, and travel in space. Critical and thought-provoking questions, such as, "Could life exist on other planets?" and "What are black holes?," are investigated through hands-on experimentation and exploration in the museum setting.

Dinosaur Camp: Students will explore the evolution and diversity of the world's dinosaurs.

Robotics: Students will design, build, and program their own robots to explore an unknown planet. Using Lego Mindstorms™ robotics kits and computers, participants will learn the principles of robotics, computer programming, and mechanical engineering.

Oceans to Ocean Life: By looking at the amazing life the oceans sustain, students will learn about the oceans' biodiversity as well as waves and currents. Activities include trying out the museum's hands-on *Exploratorium/AMNH* exhibition.

Frogs: This program includes a behind-the-scenes glimpse at the museum's exhibition of live frogs, including such rare and bizarre frogs as the flattened African clawed frog and the giant African bullfrog. Participants visit Central Park and other local habitats to learn how frogs vocalize, move, and survive in a natural setting.

OUR TAKE: Any one of these programs is a perfect start for a future student of natural history or the sciences. These programs are terrific, highly engaging, interactive, and just the sort of experience that sparks passionate pursuit. These programs are held in conjunction with a first-rate cultural institution and are a great way for your children to spend a part of their summer.

OUR RECOMMENDATION: Check out the Web site for more information on each program and prices. Chances are that there is at least one project in which your kid will be interested.

RUST COLLEGE STUDY ABROAD IN AFRICA
Study abroad
A. J. Stovall, Director
150 Rust Avenue
Holly Springs, MS 38635
(662) 252-8000
info@naaslc.org
www.naaslc.org

QUICK TAKE: Rust College, one of the oldest African American colleges in the country, offers a study abroad program that allows kids to take classes and gain college credit. This camp gives students the chance to experience the life and culture of African villages and to learn how they are affected by current social and political situations.

AGE REQUIREMENT: 15 and older.

FEES: The program costs between $2,900 and $3,500. There's an application fee of $100 and financial aid is available. Graduate and undergraduate students are both in attendance. The program welcomes Caucasian and African American students. The kids stay at hotels or in the guesthouses of a college campus. This program is in partnership with the University of Oklahoma.

SPONSORSHIP/OWNERSHIP/ACCREDITATION: Rust College

BACKGROUND: Rust College began the program began in 1992 to give kids a chance to see the history and culture of Africa.

DESCRIPTION: There is one session five-week session each year in May and June. The study abroad program is a unique opportunity to study Africa's many cultures relative to family, economics, politics, and education. This program takes place in Gambia and Ghana. Students spend five weeks studying under the tutelage of African scholars from the continent and the United States. Classes range from English literature to business and communications. There is also time for the students to engage in extracurricular activities with friends. The students can live in college dorms, local homes, or hotels as they explore the culture and language of an exotic country.

OUR TAKE: It's a great experience for any high school student. Plus, it offers college credit, which will make your student well prepared for the future college experience. Study abroad programs are on the rise, since much of the job market asks people to communicate with others from different countries.

OUR RECOMMENDATION: This program is a once in a lifetime experience that can change your child and provide him or her with an understanding of African American culture. Research the program and call the director for more information. If the program is as impressive as Mr. Stovall, it's a worthwhile experience.

INTELLECTUAL

This category is most associated with the child who is unique in thought, spirit, and personality—the kid who thinks outside the box. Often categorized as "gifted," we look at the intellectual as the kid whose pursuit is *learning;* the child who is hungry to expand his or her mind. The quest of these children is to absorb as much information as possible; these children make a sport out of intense thinking. These children are scholars, a term which has fallen by the wayside over the years. Others are "intellectual competitors" who enjoy competing against others just for the challenge of the contest.

The American Mathematics Competition is one such challenge that recognizes the mathematician as a scholar and a sportsman. They call their kids *Mathletes* or Math Athletes, and it is a program that recognizes and encourages the child with mathematical aptitude.

The Duke Tips Program is one of four Talent Identification Programs (TIPs) in the country. It provides diverse programs specially designed to meet the needs of gifted children. One of the most respected programs in the country, it focuses on intellectual programs and learning experiences for the "superintelligent" child.

AMERICAN MATHEMATICS COMPETITIONS

Steven Dunbar, Director
University of Nebraska–Lincoln
1740 Vine Street
Lincoln, NE 68588-0658
(402) 472-2257
amcinfo@unl.edu
www.unl.edu/amc

QUICK TAKE: You have to earn your way into the program by taking a series of very tough, very competitive math exams. Your child will compete against 300,000 kids to gain entry into one of thirty spots in the summer program. They, in turn, will eventually compete for one of seven spots on the international team representing the United States. This program looks for the best and brightest kids and lets them participate in "problem solving and enriching mathematics experiences."

SPONSORSHIP/OWNERSHIP/ACCREDITATION: Mathematical Association of America (MAA)

FEES: The program is free and travel is covered. Sponsors include Microsoft, the Office of Naval Research, and the Army Research Office.

AGE REQUIREMENT: Grades 9 through 12 (exceptions are made for the "super" mathematician, who can begin as early as grade 6). Admission based on the eligibility test.

BACKGROUND: Originally sponsored by the New York Metropolitan Section of the MAA, the American Mathematics Competitions started in New York City in 1950 and involved 238 schools and 6,000 students. This year, more than 413,000 students in more than 5,100 schools participated in the AMC 10/12 Contests held in February. Another 10,000 students have qualified to participate in other programs held throughout the year.

DESCRIPTION: Each year, AMC sends information about the program to every school that teaches sixth through twelfth grades. There are five contests: the AMC 8, 10, and 12 (for kids at or below those grade levels), the American Invitational Mathematics Exam (AIME), and the United States of America Mathematics Olympiad (USAMO). According to the Web site, "the AMC contests are intended for everyone from the average student at a typical school who enjoys mathematics to the very best student at the most special school." In March and April, qualifying rounds for the AIME take place, pairing a group of 10,000 students down to approximately 250. "The AMC year culminates with the Mathematical Olympiad Summer Program (MOSP) which is a four-week training program for 100 of the top qualifying AMC students. It is from this group of truly exceptional students that the U.S.A. Team, which will represent the United States at the International Mathematical Olympiad (IMO) is chosen. With state competitions, award ceremonies in Washington, DC, and international competitions, AMC stands as a neatly organized way for your math whiz to be recognized and decorated. The summer program is approximately three weeks long.

OUR TAKE: Since it's one of the most organized intellectual programs for kids out there, we give it a rave review. The fact that they send enrollment materials to all schools, from the most select private institutions to run-of-the-mill public schools, is a huge plus.

OUR RECOMMENDATION: Every school has the opportunity to get involved, so do so! It's a stellar opportunity for students with math proficiencies to use their skills in a constructive way. And who knows, with sponsors like the research coun cils of the Army and Navy as well as Microsoft, this program could be a springboard for your child's successful career.

ODYSSEY OF THE MIND

Carol Ann DeSimine, Assistant Director
Route 130 South, Suite F
Gloucester City, NJ 08030
(856) 456-7776
info@odysseyofthemind.com
www.odysseyofthemind.com

QUICK TAKE: Nation's first creative problem solving competition. The competition begins at the school level and works its way up to an international competition, which involves both domestic and foreign schools. School must be a member of "Odyssey of the Mind" (the school pays a very nominal fee for membership). Each school may have up to fourteen teams. Four thousand schools participate each year. A coach (parent or teacher) is needed for each team.

AGE REQUIREMENT: Kindergarten through grade twelve. There are four divisions: *Division I* – each team member must be under 12 years of age and in a grade no higher than 5th by May 1 of that school year. *Division II* – Kids must be younger than 15 years of age and in a grade no higher than 8th by May 1 of that school year and not be qualified for Division I. *Division III* – Kids must be in grades K–12 and not qualified for Division I or II. *Division IV* – Collegiate: Age groups overlap because the divisions are based on aptitude. Team members must be high school graduates and enrolled in at least one course at a two- or four-year college or university.

SPONSORSHIP/OWNERSHIP/ACCREDITATION: NASA is one of the sponsors and supporters of this competition.

BACKGROUND: Odyssey of the Mind, established in the early 1980s by Dr. Sam Micklus, a professor of industrial design at Rowan University (then Glassboro State College in New Jersey), introduced his students to many mind-bending engineering and mechanical projects. The local media picked up on his fun classroom atmosphere and before long, people outside the institution wanted to share the experience. Eventually, a "creative problem-solving for school children" program was born, and more than twenty years after its inception, Odyssey of the Mind has become an international program.

DESCRIPTION: Each year, kids compete on five long-term problems, selected from the following categories: (1) mechanical/vehicle—building and operating vehicles; (2) classics—books, art, and architecture; (3) performance; (4) structure—building, using only balsa wood and glue; and (5) technical performance, where kids "make innovative contraptions and incorporate artistic elements into their solutions." With problem-solving skills becoming more and more imperative in today's society, this competition is designed to help kids "think smart," "think logically," and gain proficiency in thinking through a challenge.

There are chartered associations in most areas of the country in which local competitions are held. Points are awarded and a national and international champion is determined. Kids can win educational scholarships and travel to various parts of the country and world to compete against other participants.

OUR TAKE: Overall, this competition is a good experience. It teaches team work, school spirit, and a sense of self to or the intelligent child who wants to stretch his or her mind.

OUR RECOMMENDATION: If your child's school is not already an Odyssey of the Mind member, it is probably worth looking into. For the $135 school fee, 14 teams of your school's best and brightest students can make you, your community, and themselves proud of their problem-solving abilities. If your child's school is already a member, it could be fun and character building for him/her. Even if your team doesn't skyrocket to the international competition, children will learn to think for themselves, think creatively, and make friends with kids who have similar interests.

TIPS PROGRAM
Talent identification program
Martha Putallaz, Director
Duke University Tip, Box 90780
Durham, NC 27708-0780
(919) 668-9100
information@tip.duke.edu
www.tip.duke.edu

QUICK TAKE: Is your exceptionally bright student not feeling sufficiently challenged at school? The Duke University TIPS program is world famous for enhancing the talent and intellectual skills of gifted children. This course will keep them on their toes and help them to learn more about a variety of subjects, while living in a college dorm and working on an advanced level.

AGE REQUIREMENT: Grades 7–12 (Note: There is another program for 4th and 5th graders.)

FEES: The camp is located at Duke University, the Johns Hopkins University, Northwestern University, and the University of Colorado. Tuition varies depending on the camp.

BACKGROUND: TIP was founded in 1980 by a grant to the Duke Endowment. Since then, TIP has offered programs to help find promising young students and give them the chance to expand their horizons.

DESCRIPTION: Attendees are encouraged to explore new venues of learning and discussion in intensive programs. A Summer Studies program for students in grades 7 to 10 includes 40-hour per week courses taught by instructors dedicated to this age group. The Pre-College program for 11th graders provides courses offered by Duke and taught by Duke professors, which allow students to get a more genuine feel of the college. It also offers seminars on different areas of interest that may help students decide on a career path. The Field Studies program similarly allows 10th to 12th graders to take college courses so they can get a better feel for the dedication needed to accomplish more advanced work. Along with academic courses, Duke has programs, such as a Leadership Institute, that encourages kids to help others and make new friends. Check out the Web site for more information about registration. For high school juniors and seniors, a minimum score on the PSATs is required.

OUR TAKE: This program will intellectually challenge your brilliant student to understand what's out there after high school. The in-depth courses provide students with an idea of what college is really like. This program will look great on your student's transcript when he or she is ready to apply to college. Steven Pfeiffer, one of our "eminent achievers," once ran this program, which, by the nature of its sophisticated programming and the caliber of its students, provides a life-changing experience and memory.

OUR RECOMMENDATION: This program is a slam-dunk for exceptional children. It will challenge them and encourage them to be who they are—intellectuals.

SUPERCAMP/QUANTUM LEARNING SUPERCAMP
Learning and life skills camp
Bobbi DePorter, Founder and President
Enrollments Department
SuperCamp
1725 South Coast Highway
Oceanside, CA 92054–5319
(800) 285-3276
info@supercamp.com
www.supercamp.com

QUICK TAKE: A camp that gives students' the skills to improve their academic standing when returning to the school environment, as well as the self-confidence to speak publicly and take risks. It works for the "A" student, as well as those less proficient. SuperCamp has been so well received that it is now an international camp. Learning and Life Skills are emphasized.

AGE REQUIREMENT: 11–18

FEES: The session length and prices depend on which location your student attends. Sessions usually are usually 8 to 12 days.

BACKGROUND: SuperCamp began in 1981 and provides students with the tools and strategies to improve their schoolwork. All courses are designed to give kids more self-confidence as they work harder, speak in front of peers, and make decisions. Camps can be found in Massachusetts, California, Colorado, North Carolina, Massachusetts, Hong Kong, Singapore, Mexico, Switzerland, and other locations.

DESCRIPTION: Many academic programs are offered to help students improve their study habits, memorize information faster, and write with greater ease. Other courses teach students how to study and take SAT tests so that their scores will improve. Along with study skills, the camp also helps students build their self-esteem and gives them the motivation needed to take risks as they embark on such outdoor activities as walking on a tightrope or experiencing other adventures.

OUR TAKE: This camp provides great all-around skills to all students. After speaking with Bobbi DePorter, one of the founders and President of SuperCamp, I am even more inclined to recommend the program. She believes that a child should never feel alone during this camp experience, so even shy kids can thrive here. They put kids in teams and work on drawing them out. Bobbi said kids return each year until they can participate as a teacher at the camp. Even if your kid is already smart or sociable, this camp could definitely give provide an edge in his or her work. Kids who have taken the course have found that their SAT scores improved dramatically.

OUR RECOMMENDATION: Check the Web site for locations and information on the programs, and then apply. Your student can take so much away from this experience!

U.S. CHESS CENTER SUMMER CAMPS

David Mehler, Executive Director
1501 M Street NW
Washington, DC 20005
(202) 857-4922
dmehler@chessctr.org
www.chessctr.org

QUICK TAKE: U.S. Chess Center summer camps teach more than chess, they teach camaraderie, and most importantly, different ways to have fun. A trip to Washington, DC, can become much more enriching for your child if you let him or her participate in this weekly program.

AGE REQUIREMENT: 10–14

FEES: In addition to programs at the U.S. Chess Center, there are camps at many DC area schools as well as annual weekend programs held in eight cities across the United States Prices range from $70/week to $160/week.

BACKGROUND: The U.S. Chess Center was established in 1992, three years after World Chess champion Garry Kasparov visited the nation's capital and suggested that chess could be used as a tool to fight drug use among children. That summer, fifty public housing students participated in a pilot program that drew rave reviews from the kids. Now, approximately two thousand children are involved, many from the inner city.

DESCRIPTION: The half- and full-day programs, each lasting ono wook, toach childron tho nuancos of chcoo. Thcy aloo provide swimming and other activities. In addition, some full-day camps offer an after-care problem-solving enrichment program (for an additional fee). Financial assistance is available.

OUR TAKE: Chess is one of the most stimulating games for children and adults alike, and any program geared toward teaching it while simultaneously connecting kids with their peers gets an A+ in our book. The best thing about this program is that there are enough locations, dates, and times to snugly fit into any schedule. Check out the Web site or call for specific information, but don't hesitate. Seats go fast.

OUR RECOMMENDATION: For the kid who has some competitive fire to go with his or her intellect, U.S. Chess Center summer camps are perfect. For the parent who wants to facilitate that competitive nature and intellect, they're even more perfect.

INVENTOR
Innovator, Computer Scientist/Technician

In the past ten to fifteen years, we have learned that computer innovators think differently. After the advent of the computer, a person who might previously have stayed up all night with a HAM radio, now experiments with technology and the development of software.

Computer programs and camps are run throughout the country. This section introduces a few of the better known and more respected examples. The question to ask before choosing one of these programs is, "Do you want a dedicated program, or do you want an all-around camp that also offers computer education?" Your choices are diverse and endless.

Computer Camp by Education Unlimited is a program with several locations on the West coast that offers a one-week experience for the computer innovator. This program provides a strong dose of "computer learning," but with time set aside for other activities.

Cybercamp's (Seattle, WA) philosophy is "Human brains learn more when they're having fun." This experience combines the invention, innovation, and computer innovation experience, and it recognizes that your computer whiz usually possesses talents in all three areas. The camp offers a robotic series, in which students create their own robots, as well as an arts and animation series. It's a full experience for the special child.

COMPUTER CAMP BY EDUCATION UNLIMITED
Computer camp
Matthew Fraser, Director
Education Unlimited
1700 Shattuck Ave #305
Berkeley, CA 94709
(800) 548-6612
camps@educationunlimited.com
www.educationunlimited.com

QUICK TAKE: A relaxed camp, where students are given the freedom to explore the computer. From visual to programming, your student will learn about the computer, but have time to socialize and enjoy other activities.

AGE REQUIREMENT: 10–18

DATES: The program is located in Berkeley, Los Angeles, Stanford, and San Diego, CA; and Phoenix, AZ. Each offers a different number of one-week sessions.

FEES: Prices vary with location. Financial aid is available.

SPONSORSHIP/OWNERSHIP/ACCREDITATION: Education Unlimited

BACKGROUND: The camp was created in 1995, with a program designed to help prepare students for high school and college by teaching them computer skills.

DESCRIPTION: Kids learn about programming, games, and new software as they enjoy themselves in a social camp environment. Their schedule allows time for recreational activities, including hikes, trips to zoos, and video games (varies by location).

OUR TAKE: This is a great environment, in which any kid can learn about computers. There are no grades or finals—just the enjoyment that comes from being more computer savvy.

This is a friendly, noncompetitive environment in which students can feel calm and confident in their work.

OUR RECOMMENDATION: Check out each camp location to see which will best suit your kid. The camp provides transportation to and from the airport for $45 round trip.

COMPUTER-ED HIGH-TECH CAMPS
Computer camp
Francesca Foti, Director
Somerville, MA 02145
(617) 625-2525
mfrancy@computercamps.com
www.computercamps.com

QUICK TAKE: At this camp, kids are given the tools and the opportunity to build a computer, work on computer graphics, and understand programs such as JAVA. This camp teaches how the complex machine works—and makes it look easy. Kids are guided by a brilliant and diverse staff, as they explore and gain an understanding of technology.

AGE REQUIREMENT: 8–17

DATES: The camp in Massachusetts offers four sessions every summer; the Illinois camp holds three. Sessions are from 10 to 13 days in June, July, or August.

FEES: Day program, $795 to $925; Boarding program, $1,595 to $1,700.

BACKGROUND: The camp was started in 1982 and has locations at Lasell College in Massachusetts and Lake Forest Academy in Illinois. Students come from around the world. Older students help younger campers as they work together.

DESCRIPTION: Three types of workshops are offered. In the art workshops, students study beginning to advanced computer art, graphics, and 3D modeling. The High Tech workshops give students the tools and knowledge to build a PC! Here, they also can learn about Web design, radio-controlled cars, and related technical topics. The Programming classes encompass C, C++, JAVA script, Visual Basic, and so on. Kids receive individualized training and lectures from staff members with expertise in each area. The kids are on a busy, organized schedule, but there's still time for some recreational activities as well.

OUR TAKE: This camp provides challenging and innovative work for kids young and old.

OUR RECOMMENDATION: Make sure your kid really wants to understand the nuts and bolts of computers.

CYBERCAMPS
Computer camp
Cybercamps Information Office
2401 4th Avenue, Suite 11101
Seattle, WA 98121
(206) 442-4500
info@cybercamps.com
www.cybercamps.com

QUICK TAKE: This camp is for any kid who wants to learn more about computers. It offers a wide variety of courses (from programming to visual arts) that will give your child the ability to explore all aspects of the field.

AGE REQUIREMENT: 7–18

DATE: Several sessions are held throughout the school months, as well as in the summer. Summer sessions range from 5 to 21 days in June, July, or August.

FEES: Day program, $589 to $799. Boarding program, $909 and $1,059. Financial aid is available.

BACKGROUND: An academic program started in 1997, the Cybercamps philosophy is "Human brains learn more when they're having fun." Cybercamps has locations across the nation, so there is probably one near you.

DESCRIPTION: Kids will get about five hours of hands-on work for creating new projects and learning more about technology. At the camp, kids can take one-week courses or series courses that can last for three to four weeks. Among the courses offered are a Programmer Series, in which students are taught C++ and learn about professional programming. There's also a robotic series, for students to create their own robots and later face off in a "battle-bots" tournament! The Arts and Animation Series allows students to work with digital photography and show off their artistic side. There is also time for recreational games and activities, when students get the chance to meet other campers.

OUR TAKE: This camp mixes computer skills and fun. If your child wants to become a computer whiz, this is a possibility. The multitude of courses offered attract all types of kids. Those who are in the boarding program get to experience life in a university dorm. This is a great camp, where students can enjoy themselves, broaden their knowledge of computer technology, and maybe discover their career path.

OUR RECOMMENDATION: Make sure you call to see if this camp will provide the best experience for your child. Because there are so many Cybercamps around the country, your research is important.

LEADER
Negotiator, Debater, Peacemaker

This section is for the future politician, international business leader, foreign relations specialist, corporate head, community leader, and even president of a local rotary club.

Leadership is an outstanding quality. A strong and effective leader should have excellent negotiation skills and be an effective debater, someone who gets their point across and is a good communicator. In today's world, peacemaking skills are also important for any leader. Resolving conflict is an art and a skill that can be fine tuned with training.

Presidential Classroom is a remarkable experience for a teenager. Located in Washington, DC, the program teaches the mechanics of American government. Students learn how to legislate, as they meet with members of congress and legislative officials and witness the process in action. Through direct experience and seminars, this program teaches future leaders the arts of negotiation, debating, and peacemaking, as well as other subjects essential to leadership.

The National Debate Institute offers a program dedicated to the art of debate. It is effective in teaching future leaders to think on their feet, in giving them the confidence to speak in front of a group, and in showing them how to get their points across successfully.

JUNIOR STATESMAN SUMMER SCHOOL
Government and politics camp
Preeta Nayak, Director
Junior Statesman Foundation
400 South El Camino Real
San Mateo, CA 94402
(650) 347-1600

QUICK TAKE: This camp focuses on all parts of the government. It helps kids hone their leadership skills, gain an awareness of politics, and develop their speaking skills. The camp is intense, but your kid can leave with high school credit because a few AP and Honors classes are included in the program.

AGE REQUIREMENT: 14–18

FEES: The Boarding program is $3,300, but financial aid is available.

DATE: 27 days from June to July

SPONSORSHIP/OWNERSHIP/ACCREDITATION: Stanford University

BACKGROUND: The Junior Statesman Program is held at a number of colleges, including Georgetown University in DC and Princeton University in New Jersey. The program has been active for sixty years and provides kids with an appreciation of American government, along with leadership skills needed to contribute to society.

DESCRIPTION: The curriculum is tough: classes six days a week, with AP classes in American government, economics, and comparative government. Classes are taught by professors of government, and guest speakers provide other points of view and enhance the discussion. The camp provides recreational activities, including dances for the students on weekends.

OUR TAKE: An amazing opportunity for any student with an interest in leadership and in learning more about our government. This is an excellent opportunity for the student who is up to the challenge.

OUR RECOMMENDATION: There are many excellent colleges with this program, so there's a good chance of finding one near you.

NATIONAL DEBATE INSTITUTE
Debate camp
Robert Thomas, Associate Director
California National Debate Institute
Education Unlimited
1700 Shattuck Avenue #205
Berkeley, CA
(510) 548-4800
www.educationunlimited.com

QUICK TAKE: This program is really dedicated to the improvement and development of debating skills among young adults. If your kid has an interest in law or business, this is an excellent way to learn that skill. Two simultaneous programs run over the summer, one in California at Berkeley and another on the campus of the University of Maryland. Students who attend are serious about competing in debate and are there to prepare for various national competitions,

AGE REQUIREMENT: 14–18

SPONSORSHIP/OWNERSHIP/ACCREDITATION: Public Speaking Institute

DATES: Two sessions per year, which last 14 to 18 days

FEES: Application fee, $85. University of Maryland program, $2,300; Berkeley program, $950/week. Financial aid is available.

BACKGROUND: The Public Speaking Institute began this academic program in 1995 to provide students with a greater understanding of the fundamentals of public speaking and communication skills. The Public Speaking Institute holds camps of this nature in several excellent colleges such as Stanford University, the University of California at Berkeley, where it is called the California National Debate Institute, and at the University of Maryland in College Park under the name of the National Debate Institute.

DESCRIPTION: The program is for successful students (GPA above 3.0) with a desire to understand and improve their competitive debate skills. Students will live in college housing and experience the competitive atmosphere at this higher level of learning. The topics range from ecology and politics to philosophy and government.

OUR TAKE: Although this is a great program for the child considering competitive debating or a career in law or business, every child will benefit from learning these skills. If a kid is committed to overcoming shyness, this program might be the answer, but note that these debate devotees take it very seriously. Most professionals require strong speaking skills and the ability to speak effectively in front of large groups. This program is an excellent way to hone the skills necessary to craft a debating position and develop more fluid speech.

OUR RECOMMENDATION: The camp will definitely be a positive on college applications, but, more importantly, it will test children's thinking skills as well as their abilities as debaters. It can be a very positive experience for the prepared student.

PRESIDENTIAL CLASSROOM

Jann Hoag, Vice President of Programs
119 Oronoco Street
Alexandria, VA 22314-2015
(800) 441-6433
info@presidentialclassroom.org

QUICK TAKE: This program is for students interested in the mechanics of American government. Presidential Classroom provides the exemplary student with the opportunity to spend a week in Washington, DC, with more access to government institutions than is usually afforded

AGE REQUIREMENT: The student must be a high school junior or a senior, with either a B average or a ranking in the top 25% of his/her class. One-week programs are offered from January to March and in June and July.

BACKGROUND OF THE PROGRAM: Presidential Classroom is based on a series of educational initiatives implemented by leaders in Washington, DC, who were interested in challenging American youth. President John F. Kennedy initiated the first programs in the two series: "Widening Horizons" and the "White House Seminars." Vice President Hubert Humphrey followed with "Washington Briefings." The success of the programs and the increasing number of young people who wished to be involved led to the charter of the Presidential Classroom in 1968. Students are housed at Georgetown University, where they meet in the Conference Center. Seminars are held in notable government institutions all over our Nation's Capitol.

DESCRIPTION: The program's motto is "Not Your Typical Week in Washington," and through its well-established relationships with different parts of the Federal government, the Presidential Classroom ensures the week will be anything but typical. Students visit the House and Senate floors and various embassies, receive a CIA briefing, and gain access to the State Department. Locations vary according to which program is chosen. The original scholars' program has been augmented with at least six special seminars that concentrate on specific topics (such as national security, science/technology, and public policy) that explore the relationship of these subjects to government policy. Not just an all-access tour of our nation's capital, but a gathering of leaders among students from all around the country, Presidential Classroom allows for a significant amount of peer exchange within a formidable setting.

OUR TAKE: Presidential Classroom is an exceptional way of bringing the study of government to life. Apart from the visits to government offices and institutions, students participate in a mock presidential election and debate domestic and international issues. These forms of peer exchange, in addition to the many private conversations among students, encourage the development of self-confidence, esteem, and communication skills. Another impressive feature of Presidential Classroom—one that has a profound effect on the kids—is the appointment set up between the students and their member of congress. There is no better way for a student to understand that our government is operated "by the People" and "for the People."

OUR RECOMMENDATION: This program is exceptional for the following reasons: peer exchange; student participation in debates, lectures, and programs that are designed to illustrate and give students a "hands-on" feeling for the way government works; personal interaction with government officials, and visits to the formidable offices and buildings of our nation's capital. It teaches students negotiation "first-hand" by a free and equal exchange of ideas through mock summits. Presidential Classroom is the best way to give a kid a sense of what "national leadership" entails. The downside is that the programs only last one week.

NATURALIST
Outdoor Adventurer, Explorer

L earning to master the environment requires cooperation, physical ability, discipline, and knowledge. The programs included in this section teach the skills essential to survival. These courses test kids to the limit, and children are expected to push themselves and perform.

NOLS (National Outdoor Leadership Skills), one of the country's most respected programs, is located at the site where NASA trains its astronauts. Ocean Classroom is a program that teaches kids how to live on the ocean and operate a boat, at the same time as students complete the equivalent of a semester in high school.

In outdoor programs, kids are taught to work as a group and rely on one another. At the same time they learn respect, camaraderie, friendship, and an appreciation for the environment. Such programs help children gain maturity, but it takes a certain type of child to do well.

EARTHWATCH INSTITUTE
Ecology, Archeology, Zoology, World Health Programs
John Walker, Principal
3 Clock Tower Place, Suite 100
Maynard, MA 01754
(800) 776-0188 ext. 218 or (978) 450-1268
studentinfo@earthwatch.org
www.earthwatch.org

QUICK TAKE: With 3,500 members volunteering their time and skills to work with 120 research scientists each year on field projects in more than 50 countries, Earthwatch Institute is an intense educational program that seeks to promote an understanding of the actions necessary to sustain the natural environment. Conversation, research, and education about the world we live in and the effect of the environment on our daily lives is researched and explored.

AGE REQUIREMENT: Volunteers must be at least 16 years old for most programs; a few expeditions require volunteers to be at least 18 or 21 years old. Participation by minors (ages 16 and 17) is usually limited to two per team to help manage group dynamics on research expeditions.

FEES: $700 to $4,000 per person, excluding travel to and from the rendezvous. The price of each project covers food, accommodations, on-site travel, and all costs of field research (field permits, equipment, etc.). There are student grants and fellowships are available for advanced students who are nominated.

BACKGROUND: The Earthwatch Institute is an international not-for-profit organization founded in Boston, with offices in Oxford, England; Melbourne, Australia; and Tokyo, Japan. There are 50,000 members and supporters throughout Europe, Africa, Asia, and Australia.

DESCRIPTION: The Earthwatch Institute has a variety of field research and educational opportunities in the United States and abroad. These expeditions allow your teenager to work hands-on with a scientist in the field and gain valuable first-hand knowledge about techniques in data collection, awareness of environmental issues, exploration of new cultures and environments, and many personal growth topics. According to its Web site, Earthwatch expeditions are ongoing research projects confronting critical, current issues, run by qualified and respected members of the scientific community. Earthwatch expeditions are short-term volunteer opportunities directly assisting scientists in their field research. Most projects last 10 to 14 days, but one-week, three-week, and weekend opportunities are also available. The researchers come from all over the globe. The Web page includes quotations from past students that give a good idea of the quality and intensity of the Earthwatch experience: http://www.earthwatch .org/education/student/scap/student_quotes.html.

OUR TAKE: With forays into the science of discovery and objective knowledge about the environment, this program and experience has the potential to be life changing.

OUR RECOMMENDATION: This is a terrific way to enhance the personal growth process by increasing self-confidence, environmental awareness, a sense of community, and a sense of self. The students should be mature, team players, and willing to immerse themselves in the program. A strong experience for the right kid.

ENVIRONMENTAL STUDIES SEMINAR
YOUTH INSTITUTE
Environmental camp
Brooks McKinney, Director
Hobart and William Smith Colleges
Geneva, NY 14456
(315) 781-3819
jbmck@hws.edu
www.hws.edu/aca/enviro/

QUICK TAKE: A camp for kids who love research and are eager to understand more about the environment. College professors conduct the program, and the students receive all the tools necessary to perform research in the Seneca Lake area. College credit is offered to those who successfully complete the camp.

AGE REQUIREMENT: 16–18

DATE: Two weeks in July

FEES: Application fee, $25; boarding program, $1,700. Financial aid is available.

SPONSORSHIP/OWNERSHIP/ACCREDITATION: Hobart and William Smith Colleges

BACKGROUND: The program was founded in 1993 by a group of professors focused on environmental issues.

DESCRIPTION: Students work in the field, on the lake, or in laboratories conducting research on the area. An oceanographic vessel (the HWS Explorer) is used to explore Seneca Lake and nearby nature preserves. Experiment stations also add to the experience. Seminars are taught on subjects that range from environmental policy and politics to nature photography and literature related to the environment. All classes are taught by college professors. The program also offers camping trips to the Adirondack Mountains for additional research opportunities.

OUR TAKE ON THE PROGRAM: A really special experience for those with an interest in the environment. The curriculum is difficult, but rewarding.

OUR RECOMMENDATION: This camp, which really focuses on all aspects of the environment, is a great opportunity for any high school student who has an interest in the natural environment. Transportation to the campus can be arranged from airports in Rochester, Syracuse, and Ithaca, New York ($50 each way).

(NOLS) NATIONAL OUTDOOR LEADERSHIP SCHOOL
Outdoor Adventure through Leadership Program
Bruce Palmer, Director of Admissions
284 Lincoln Street
Lander, WY 82520-2848
(800) 710-NOLS
admissions@nols.edu
www.nols.edu

QUICK TAKE: This program is for the child who is serious about the outdoors. To be accepted, children must be in good physical shape. NOLS is dedicated to risk management, but there is risk involved. These adventures require that children test their limits and raise their personal bar of accomplishment.

AGE REQUIREMENT: 14 and older

FEES: Call for information.

BACKGROUND: The National Outdoor Leadership School (NOLS), a not-for-profit educational program, was established in 1965, one year after the "Wilderness Act" became law. Paul Petzolt, a legendary mountaineer, world famous climber, and member of the Army's 10th mountain division, started NOLS to train leaders to master the outdoors and to learn about, protect, and care for the wilderness. He wanted to provide people with the tools to travel through wild places and not only survive, but thrive. Today, NASA trains astronauts here.

DESCRIPTION: Classes are organized by age (14 and 15, 16, 17, 18–24), held in the summer, and last either 14 or 28 days. On- and off-trail hiking, introduction to rock climbing, peak ascents, and negotiating boulder fields with a 50-pound backpack along a 75-mile hiking route are all part of the Wyoming

Adventure for 14 and 15 year olds, which takes a group of approximately eight children and two instructors to elevations of 7,000 to 13,000 feet. (The number of students and instructors varies depending on the program.) Kids will learn outdoor living skills, how to get along with other members of their group, and how to be a leader even when they are in the back of the pack.

OUR TAKE: This program can positively impact a child's life in many quantifiable and nonquantifiable ways. Kids return home sure of their abilities and with a strong sense of self, but it is not appropriate for every child. Your child must be physically and emotionally prepared for the program and must be motivated. Students come from all backgrounds and with different levels of experience. The desire to learn and participate is the most important factor for success on a NOLS course.

OUR RECOMMENDATION: This is an amazing course—it builds character, is life changing, and offers incredible adventure—and NOLS fastidiously practices risk management, but *there are risks.* Parents, do your homework, do your research, and know your child. This is a serious decision and must be a joint one between parent and child.

OCEAN CLASSROOM
Ocean camp
Bert Rogers, Executive Director
Ocean Classroom Foundation
PO Box 446
Cornwall, NY 12518
(800) 724-7245
mail@oceanclassroom.org
www.oceanclassroom.org

QUICK TAKE: This award-winning program takes place on water and is so full of information that it is the equivalent of a high school semester. Young adults take the reins in learning how to operate a boat, while keeping up with the studies they would be taking at their high schools. It's character building, challenging, demanding, and exciting. The result is an experience that enables children to realize their abilities and to develop a sense of self-confidence that will stay with them throughout life. What makes this program even more exciting are the "awesome" locations one can choose to explore. This is an amazing experience for any student with real dreams of maritime pursuits or a student with a sense of adventure who enjoys a significant challenge.

SPONSORSHIP/OWNERSHIP/ACCREDITATION: Sponsored by: Ocean Classroom Foundation. Accredited by: Proctor Academy of Andover, NH.

AGE REQUIREMENT: 15–18 (there are other programs for 13–16 year olds and college undergraduates)

ADDITIONAL INFORMATION: Although the main contact is in New York, the locations range from the Bahamas, Cuba, and the Dominican Republic to Haiti, Puerto Rico, and elsewhere.

DATES: 3 sessions, each lasting between 63 and 120 days, are offered in every month but December.

FEES: The cost is a hefty, $6,950–$12,750. Financial aid is available.

BACKGROUND: This not-for-profit foundation began the program in 1994 to teach students about the sea and navigation. It provides a challenging experience and a vigorous academic program in maritime studies.

DESCRIPTION: The Ocean Classroom is the equivalent of a high school semester. It offers the same subjects, but they are uniquely designed to revolve around the sea. For example, marine science, marine history, marine applied mathematics, and so on. Focus is on all aspects of the sea, including the exploration of ocean ecosystems in some of the most beautiful places on earth. The really remarkable aspect of this camp is that students get the chance to operate the boats, while achieving a level of responsibility and maturity well beyond their years. The selection process is rigid; an interview is required. There is an adjustment involved; the optimal candidate must be able to manage a day filled with the challenges of being at sea at the same time as he or she keeps up academically. The program is equally divided between male/female participation and Bert Rogers, the executive director, says both do equally well in this program.

OUR TAKE: This is an amazing, unparalleled course of study that is packed with activity and the challenge/responsibility of operating a boat. When asked about the social side of the program and if the kids get along, we were told that the demands of the program and the ocean were a great leveler and led to camaraderie. The kids learn to operate as a group and rely on each other, which helps build respect and friendship. The Ocean Classroom takes place during the school year, and students receive high school credit (some programs give college credit). Not only are the students involved in the work, they are also learning the process while getting hands-on experience. The exotic locations allow students to closely observe habitats that can't be seen in the United States. This is an excellent program for kids interested in the sea, but our feeling is that it is a life-changing program for any student who can meet this kind of challenge.

OUR RECOMMENDATION: This is one that is awe inspiring, and we recommend it wholeheartedly for the kid who has the energy, drive, interest, commitment, and responsibility to meet this challenge. The only drawback is: how does a child return to school after participating in it? Two to three months at sea can either be a very short time or very long time depending on the child. This is why the Ocean Classroom's selection process is so discerning. For the kids who participate, these months will pass quickly but always be remembered.

OUTWARD BOUND
Adventure, Nature, and Leadership Camp
John Underhill, Director of Admissions
100 Mystery Point Road
Garrison, NY 10524
(866) 467-7651
OBNDev@outwardbound.org
www.outwardbound.org

QUICK TAKE: This program was created for those who appreciate the outdoors and wish to share their experiences with like-minded individuals. Outward Bound is primarily an athletic program in the United States and around the world with a philosophy that emphasizes personal growth through experience and challenges in the wilderness, urban settings, boardrooms, and classrooms. It offers children a chance to not only gain knowledge of various outdoor skills, but also to gain knowledge of themselves.

AGE REQUIREMENT: 12 and older

FEES: C Courses run year-round and range from 7 to 85 days. International courses are also offered in at least 28 foreign countries.

BACKGROUND: Outward Bound was established during World War II through the combined efforts of Sir Lawrence Holt, a British shipping tycoon, and Kurt Hahn, a progressive German educator, to instruct young sailors in sea survival skills. In the 1950s, Josh Miner, an American who taught under Hahn at the Gordonstoun School in Scotland, was inspired by Hahn's emphasis on team building and founded the Outward Bound movement in the United States. Expeditionary learning, the philosophy upon which Outward Bound is based, is a model for school reform and is utilized in more than 1,000 schools and universities in the United States. It is a whole-school reform model for K–12 schools that uses active learning to help students develop character as well as achieve academic success.

DESCRIPTION: Mountaineering, snowboarding, rock climbing, white water rafting, desert backpacking, dog-sledding—certainly not the list of activities at your average sleep-away camp—are among the programs offered. The program focuses on intensive activities that help students develop a strong sense of self within a team setting. Through detail-oriented activities, such as sailing, the program ensures character development as a child strives to meet the ever-increasing demands of each activity and, under the supervision of an experienced instructor, begins to recognize his/her self-imposed limits and then concentrates on overcoming them. Outward Bound believes that character development is contingent upon a sense of social and environmental responsibility and therefore it includes volunteer work (e.g., shoreline clean-up, trail maintenance, and community assistance) as a means of instilling the values of stewardship.

OUR TAKE: Outward Bound truly recognizes the full value of physical activity and does not merely practice it for its own sake. I am confident that the program "practices what it preaches." Outward Bound's philosophy is increasingly employed in academic settings, with a high success rate (as assessed independently by researchers of alternative educational methods).

OUR RECOMMENDATION: When considering such an intensely physical program as Outward Bound, safety must be the primary concern. While participation implies a certain amount of risk, the instructors (who are either certified in Wilderness Advanced First Aid, as Wilderness First Responders, or as Emergency Medical Technicians) undergo regular safety training. Independent experts of national safety review teams inspect each program and course area for possible hazards. According to the insurer of Outward Bound, its rate of injury and illness is "lower than that of many other industries." This is not the program for every child; children who participate must truly desire it.

OBSERVER
Writer

Some children are born leaders; others are born observers. The born observers are the children who do more watching than talking. They observe people, events, and the world, and draw conclusions.

Great writers are usually astute observers. Writing provides children who think outside the box with an outlet for ideas, a place to record their observations, and a way to express their feelings.

Duke University, through its TIPS (Talent Identification Program) program, offers a "Young Writer's Program," which gives students an opportunity to explore their creative genius and encourages the advancement of their skills through programs in playwriting, journalism, and the writing of reviews.

The Alfred University Summer Institute in Writing and the Choate Rosemary Hall Young Writers Workshop are also programs in which kids can perfect their writing through workshops and seminars.

For your child who is the observer, a writing program may be just the thing, but remember that strong and effective writing skills are important to just about every profession. Most importantly, writing illustrates the observations of your child in a concrete way. When observations are put on paper, an idea is brought to life.

ALFRED UNIVERSITY SUMMER INSTITUTE IN WRITING
Writing camp
Melody McLay, Director
Office of Summer Programs
1 Saxon Drive
Alfred, NY 14802-1205
(607) 871-2612
summerpro@alfred.edu
www.alfred.edu/summer

QUICK TAKE: An intensive program that helps young adults improve and develop writing skills. Located in the beautiful town of Alfred in upstate New York, is a great opportunity for your student to begin searching for college. Students experience the college environment and dorm life first hand.

AGE REQUIREMENT: 15–17

FEES: Application fee, $75 (deadline, May 24); boarding fee, $395–$425.

DATES: One session of 5 days in June or July

BACKGROUND: In 2000, the university decided to expand its offerings by holding summer camps for young adults who will soon be prospective college students.

DESCRIPTION: The program at Alfred University gives young adults the opportunity to improve their writing through lectures and workshops. The program also delves into reading and text analysis. A strong program in creative writing is also offered. The goal is to create well-written work suitable for high school, and even college, courses. Your teenager will have time for recreational activities and a chance to meet fellow students. This writing program is but one of the many programs offered at Alfred University. It also provide camps in astronomy, art and design, and music. There are job opportunities for writers aged nineteen and older.

OUR TAKE: Alfred University is located in a safe, picturesque area, but it is a bit far from the airport (Rochester International Airport is 65 miles away). Transportation can be provided (although there is a charge) by the university. Your child will be challenged in the art of writing and in the revision of original work. This program would be suitable for great writers, or those who want to become a more mature writer.

OUR RECOMMENDATION: This is a serious program. RAs (resident advisers) are with the kids for the week and work to make it a social as well as a learning experience. Because writing is a skill needed in today's job market, every student will benefit from the opportunity to hone his or her skills.

CHOATE ROSEMARY HALL YOUNG WRITERS WORKSHOP
English and journalism program
Mariann Arnold, Asst. Director
Choate Rosemary Hall Summer Programs
Christian Street
Wallingford, CT 06492
(203) 697-2365
marnold@choate.edu
www.choate.edu/summer

QUICK TAKE: A writing camp for students in middle and upper school, Choate Rosemary Hall is dedicated to improving the writing skills of students, while providing an opportunity to make new friends. There is equal time for work and play, but every day is full of fun activities.

AGE REQUIREMENT: 11–14

FEES: Application fee, $60. Day program, $1,390; boarding program is $1,835. Financial aid is available. Two two-week sessions are held every year.

BACKGROUND: This program, which began in 1916, is considered quite strong. Since its inception, it has held summer camps for young adults who are interested in enhancing their academic skills. The Young Writers Workshop began in 1997 to give preteens a chance to participate in a creative writing and social environment.

DESCRIPTION: Students participate in discussions and work on exercises to improve their writing. Working with their peers, students gain the confidence to show their work to others and learn helpful techniques from one another. The program has a regimented schedule, but allows time for extracurricular activities, such as athletics or social events, which allow your child to interact with other students. There also are field trips to Boston, New York City, malls, movies, and college campuses.

OUR TAKE: The kids attend class six days a week. Wednesdays and Saturdays are half-days set aside for socializing. A RA initiates and supervises these activities. This is not a camp, but an academic program, so be prepared. If you're into writing and some fun, in that order, then this program could work for you. Your child should be relatively independent to get the most from the program.

OUR RECOMMENDATION: For children who are serious about writing, this program works. This is a great way for students to find new friends with similar interests while they hone their writing skills. All students can benefit from writing classes, and this program allows your kid to do it in an enjoyable environment.

DUKE YOUNG WRITER'S CAMP
Sarah Collie, Director
Duke University TIP
Box 90780
Durham, NC 27708
(919) 684-2827 or (919) 684-6259
scollie@duke.edu
www.learnmore.duke.edu/youth

QUICK TAKE: The Duke University Talent Identification Program is world renowned for its camps for very bright kids. This reputation is well deserved. Its writing camp is one of the strongest in the United States. Your student will have the opportunity to improve writing skills, explore types of writing, and meet kids from around the nation. This is definitely a camp for kids who are above average academically.

AGE REQUIREMENT: 12–17

FEES: Day program, $675. Boarding program, $1,395–$1,425. Three sessions over the summer, each of which lasts for 11 to 12 days.

BACKGROUND: The Young Writer's Camp was founded in 1983 at Duke University to give advanced young adults the opportunity to improve their writing skills. The focus is on journalism and communications.

DESCRIPTION: The program allows students to explore writing for different media, such as the theater, newspapers, and reviews. Students have the freedom to be creative and are encouraged to push their writing skills. Students live at Duke University and work with other students in the diverse community. The counselors are helpful and supportive of your student's development. When your child isn't writing, there are many evening and weekend recreational activities, such as arts and crafts and talent shows.

OUR TAKE: This is a great opportunity for any kid who aspires to become a writer or journalist. The Duke University TIPS Program has made a science out of creating and implementing meaningful, engrossing, educational, and inspiring programs that emphasize the "full experience," and this program has accomplished what it set out to do.

OUR RECOMMENDATION: The camp is for kids with strong, above-average grades. If your child fits the bill, this will be an amazing experience.

SCIENTIST

Rocketry and astronomy are becoming hip hobbies. The hobby of rocketry is growing by leaps and bounds, and earning a high-powered rocket license is not unusual for the rocket enthusiast. Television channels now regularly broadcast documentaries on the subject, and some traditional summer camps now place rocketry among their offerings. It is also a hobby that attracts the "out-of-the-box" thinker.

The sciences encourage children to think about how we got here and how the earth was formed. Although the issues are far greater than the young child can understand, it does make them wonder; it pushes the child to ask larger questions than they can answer. The sciences keep a child interested and engaged.

This section has programs and information that will provide guidance for those who want to become involved in astronomy, rocketry, or other science hobbies.

ASTROCAMP (GUIDED DISCOVERIES)
Astronomy camp
Ann Commetti, Registrar
Kristi & Ross Turner, Directors
P.O. Box 3399
Idyllwild, CA 92549-3399
(800) 645-1423
www.guideddiscoveries.org

QUICK TAKE: This camp offers one- and two-week summer programs for kids throughout the world who are future astronomers or who dream about "space and the universe." The facility is also available to school groups for three-day programs during the school year.

AGE REQUIREMENT: 8–14 for the one week program; 10–15 for the two week program.

FEES: One week program, $750 + $25 for airport transport; two week program, $1,500 + $25 for airport transport.

BACKGROUND: Astrocamp was founded in 1989 by Kristi and Ross Turner, the founders of Catalina Sea Camps, which are now part of Guided Discoveries. The Turners were teachers who wanted to get kids excited about science and the environment. They felt that the process of exploring created magic and that the student's discoveries would have life-long benefits. The camp is located high in the San Gabriel Mountains in California where kids can get a stellar view of the universe.

DESCRIPTION: The one-week program curriculum is very structured, with no choices available. The two-week program offers a curriculum filled with activity and course choices. Qualified instructors, including teachers, astronomers, and scientists, are the first part of the equation at Astrocamp. Among the excellent courses are rocketry; the study of electricity through the use of magnets; and hands-on-labs in astronomy, physics, lights and lasers, weather and atmosphere, geology, the solar system, and space technology. Adventure activities include high and low ropes courses, the climbing wall, bouldering, the human gyroscope, space ball, and Newton's chair. The Mission Lab guides students on simulated explorations of a newly discovered planet in the solar system. The thrill of discovery and teamwork are emphasized. This is an outstanding experience.

OUR TAKE: This camp is committed to its goal of providing a "life-enhancing" experience for those children who are avidly interested in space exploration. The staff is employed year-round, which is a definite plus, and they are trained to relate to and teach kids about the universe. Another plus is that this camp attracts kids with the same interests. This camp can provide an amazing experience for kids who want to explore space, the sky, the stars, and all that this implies.

OUR RECOMMENDATION: This is a great experience for children who are independent and passionate in their pursuit of astronomy. Being on top of a mountain, with telescopes and other equipment studying the universe, is what this camp is all about. The camp philosophy also emphasizes the social aspect of camp through an important mix of programs.

ASTRONOMY CLUBS

Local astronomy clubs are well-organized, can be found in every state, and are available to children of all ages. The American Association of Amateur Astronomers Web site, www.corvus.com, is a starting point for locating a club in your area.

The local astronomy club provides an affordable and interactive outlet for children who are interested in the cosmos. They will find kids with similar likes, or they can explore the universe with a parent or sibling. One of the most exciting events is a "Star Party." No, there are no movie stars here, but there are many telescopes—sophisticated and simple, large and small—that everyone shares to view the heavens. The Star Party lasts approximately two days and is held on a weekend when there is no moon. The sky is pitch black and the stars are so bright that you feel you are right up there with them. Attendees pitch tents and spend the evenings talking to each other; plotting astral movements and viewing moons, stars, and planets. During the day, there is some rest, activities for the kids, and discussions about the universe and upcoming astral phenomena.

For the kid who is into astronomy, this weekend is not to be taken lightly: the adults are serious about their interest and are committed to teaching and sharing what they know. Your children will meet other kids with the same interests, and, most importantly, they can immerse themselves in their hobby.

Contact your local astronomy club for more information. Some events are held on a larger scale, and some are on a smaller scale. But if you want to encourage your future astronomer, this could be the right place to begin.

The Rockland Astronomy Club is one club that receives great reviews from amateur astronomers in terms of programming and events for both children and adults. It is a club that has a huge symposium once a year: NASA representatives and former astronauts give lectures and present interactive displays for hands-on learning. Games, raffles, books, and equipment are available for sale. This club is helpful, informative, and if contacted by e-mail it will provide helpful information to interested future astronomers.

ROCKLAND ASTRONOMY CLUB
Astronomy club
Don Urban, Director
73 Haring Street
Closter, NJ 07624
(201) 768-6575
durban@rocklandastronomy.com
www.rocklandastronomy.com

QUICK TAKE: Families can join the Rockland Astronomy Club regardless of their knowledge level, making it a learning experience for the entire family.

AGE REQUIREMENT: All ages.

FEES: Annual dues are $28 for students under 19 and $48 for the family (Deduct $18 if you choose to receive information via e-mail rather than paper mail.) Application forms are on the Web site. Star Party: $35/adult, $20/kid 11–17 and $10/kid 6–10.

BACKGROUND: The Rockland Astronomy Club was founded in 1958 and provides an exciting array of activities not available elsewhere. It is a portal to the wonders of the universe through the largest and most exciting astronomy show in the United States offering outstanding lectures, workshops, star parties, planetarium shows, films, and much, much more.

DESCRIPTION: From the club's Web site: "In addition to scheduled observing activities, we hold periodic indoor meetings at various locations in Rockland County where programs are presented that focus on specific aspects of Astronomy. Among the most popular are topics relating to the purchase and use of astronomical telescopes—where to find them, what to look for, and which ones to avoid. Other subjects deal with basic celestial navigation, how to read star charts, and learning how to locate and identify galaxies, nebulae and star clusters that are generally not visible to the naked eye." Each year, the club holds its very own "Summer Star Party and Family Camping Vacation" for a week in Massachusetts' beautiful Berkshire Mountains. Each spring, the Rockland Astronomy Club sponsors a Spring Northeast Astronomy Forum and Telescope Show in Suffern, NY. Lectures are given by astronauts and other professionals. The club also organizes a variety of other programs.

OUR TAKE: The fact that they have their very own star party is a huge plus. Monthly "joy of the universe" public star parties, held in conjunction with the Palisades Interstate Parks Commission at Anthony Wayne State Park from April to October, are another highlight of this program. For father and son, mother and daughter, or even the whole family, partaking in any portion of this program—whether it is the one-week vacation or the telescope show—will give everyone lasting memories.

OUR RECOMMENDATION: It's an East Coast thing, but it's known on both coasts as one of the better astronomy programs in the country. Most clubs charge a small membership fee that enables you to take advantage of your kid's (and your) astronomy fascination. If you're looking for something unique at a uniquely reasonable cost, you're looking for the Rockland Astronomy Club.

ROCKETRY CLUBS

This exciting hobby gives you a feel for the technology used by NASA in launching rockets. It is a rapidly growing hobby that has been given a lot of press lately, with regularly aired documentary specials on the Discovery Channel. Participating in a rocketry club is an opportunity for a parent and child to work together on a joint hobby, building and launching high-powered rockets. Rocketry is an educational, safe, and exciting hobby, which is enjoyed by thousands worldwide.

Through your local rocketry club, adults and children can safely learn the science behind launching and building rockets. The clubs provide experts who pass on knowledge essential to successfully making your rocket-launching hobby more than just a day in the schoolyard, launching and losing model rockets that were purchased in the local hobby store.

There are organized launches set up all over the country. These launches provide the structure and safety essential to making this an exciting hobby. Most enthusiasts begin with a small rocket and build from there. This hobby has little competition, because once you look around and see larger rockets to your left and right, you feel compelled to size up.

You and your child will also meet other expert amateurs. Discovery television network recently produced and aired a documentary on this rapidly growing hobby.

To locate the Rocketry Club near you, go on-line to www.tripoli.org, which lists clubs all over the country. Tripoli does hold a major launch once a year, but the smaller local launches are just as much fun and a little less intimidating.

NATIONAL ASSOCIATION OF ROCKETRY–STUDENT EXPERIMENTAL PAYLOAD PROGRAM

www.nar.org/nareduc.html

QUICK TAKE: Calling all future space cadets and NASA scientists. Here's your first major assignment, a chance to be the inventor of your own rocket! Open to all kids who have the drive and determination to see their work literally soar! Plus, they will receive useful knowledge about the project. This program is definitely a dream come true for the science whiz!

AGE REQUIREMENT: All ages

BACKGROUND: A part of the educational services provided by the National Association of Rocketry, the Student Experimental Payload Program (SEP) was founded as a not-for-profit in 1990. SEP has helped launch countless experimental payload rockets, provided teacher workshops, and performed rocketry demonstrations across the United States.

DESCRIPTION: Providing hands-on experience in the field of aerospace technology, this program offers the stimulation of concepts and techniques utilized in advanced science and math.

Following the guidelines of scientific research and using the scientific method from initial concept to complete payload, the children are asked to construct a rocket that can carry a standardized payload provided by the SEP. Taking into consideration many different parameters of rocketry, they are required to track and monitor every stage of the launch, from preliminary design to post-flight evaluation.

OUR TAKE: Every child has looked skyward and thought about what's up there and how things get into the sky. With rockets capable of reaching 3,000 to 10,000 feet, this is an ideal way for your child to investigate those questions. What could be more fun than blasting off something much heftier than a bottle rocket, and knowing the why and how it all works?

OUR RECOMMENDATION: Buzz Aldrin, Neil Armstrong, and William Pickering all began by planning, experimenting, and realizing their dreams on the ground. This is a perfect opportunity for your child to begin to aim skyward, blast off, and explore some new space. Working together with other kids will also give your child the chance to make new friends with similar interests.

SCIENCE QUEST
Science program for girls
Seton Hill University
1 Seton Hill Drive
Greensburg, PA, 15601
(724) 830-1044 (tel.)
(724) 830-1571 (fax.)
yochum@setonhill.edu

QUICK TAKE: Grab your white coat and microscope. This all-girls program allows you to experience what's happening at the core of laboratory sciences. A week-long, hands-on lab experience is bolstered by field trips, women-in-science guest speakers, and recreational activities. Students work in the biology, chemistry, and computer labs of Seton Hall University.

AGE REQUIREMENT: Science Quest I: girls entering grades 7–9; Science Quest II: girls entering grades 10–12.

FEES: Call for information.

BACKGROUND: Science Quest is located in Greensburg, PA, at Seton Hall University.

DESCRIPTION: With an intensive dose of math and sciences, Science Quest participants will spend a week in the biology, chemistry, or computer labs of Seton Hall University. Each program participant becomes a member of an "expert group" and via a team approach investigates themes in biology, chemistry, forensic sciences, and nutrition. Hands-on experiments are conducted in the labs. Students learn what science has to do with what we eat and wear, how science affects our environment, and other similar topics. Women scientists give talks on the use of science in their professions.

Science Quest I is geared toward girls who are entering grades 7–9; while Science Quest II, with a more advanced approach to the various sciences, is designed for girls who are entering grades 10–12. There is also dormitory life with plenty of opportunities for recreational activities, such as swimming, hanging out with friends, playing games, and so on.

OUR TAKE: These programs offer high quality, hands-on experiences in the various laboratory sciences. Science Quest I offers something most middle-school students don't have, which is access to college-level labs. Science Quest II affords high school students the opportunity to strengthen their laboratory experience, and receive exposure to different and new fields,. The emphasis on women in science can definitely have a positive effect on your daughter's interest in, passion for, and pursuit of success in the health and life sciences.

OUR RECOMMENDATION: Future Marie Curies can a get a good head start here.

U.S. SPACE CAMP/ U.S. SPACE ACADEMY

Space adventure camp

Reservations Department
PO Box 070015
Huntsville, AL 35807-015
(800) 637-7223
info@spacecamp.com
www.spacecamp.com

QUICK TAKE: The U.S. Space Camp is a life-changing experience. This program challenges kids and parents of all ages to meet the challenges NASA astronauts face in a simulated environment. Although this program offers kids and parents a good time, it is also mind expanding with a great staff, program, and mission. Almost every kid dreams at one time or another of becoming an astronaut, and the U.S. Space Camp fulfills that dream, if for only a week or a weekend.

AGE REQUIREMENT: Children must be in the 4th grade and at least 9 years of age (7 if with a parent). The Space Academy offers classes for older students ages 12–14, and the Advanced Space Academy is for students ages 15–18. There are also parent/child weekend programs and adult/ teacher programs.

DATES: The programs are year-round and can run 3, 5, or 7 days.

FEES: $749 per person for the 5-day program. This does not include transportation costs.

SPONSORSHIP/OWNERSHIP/ACCREDITATION: Operated jointly by the U.S. Space & Rocket Center and the Alabama Space Science Exhibit Commission. Accredited by the American Camping Association.

BACKGROUND: The U.S. Space Camp was established in 1982 and has the largest number of graduated campers (almost 300,000) in the United States.

DESCRIPTION: Space Camp (ages 9–11), Space Academy (Ages 12–14), Advanced Space Academy (Ages 16–18), and Parent/Child Space Camp (Ages 7–11) offer a variety programs for kids who are interested in experiencing a taste of what is involved in an astronaut training program. The programs are typically five to six days, but there are two-day programs for parents and children who want to go through the program together. There is a sister program called the Aviation Challenge which provides a comparable experience in the field of aviation.

The program reproduces real astronaut training, including such activities as simulated Space Shuttle missions, training simulators, rocket building and launching, and lectures about the past, present, and future of space exploration.

There is also the Parent/Child Plus program, which allows more than one parent and child to participate in the program. And for mothers and daughters who do not want a co-ed experience, the Sally Ride Space Camp for mothers and daughters was established.

OUR TAKE: This camp offers simulated space missions, "spacecraft accommodations," and an attitude that is smart, motivating, and encouraging. The experience is incomparable. Space camp can help make one of your child's brightest, far-reaching dreams come true. Not only will they be doing something they want to do, but they will be living, breathing, and *eating* the "Space" experience. They will receive a hands-on education that the traditional astronomy/space curriculum in school can't provide. The facts and information learned at the U.S. Space Camp will stick in children's minds for the rest of their lives. They will learn a new way to retain information that can only help them in all future endeavors.

OUR RECOMMENDATION: Tom Hanks, Ron Howard, and the other participants in the *Apollo 13* film trained at the U.S.

Space Camp facility because of its authentic simulation of space training. If you're star struck, you might be impressed, but it's the quality of the staff, the magic, and integrity of the experience that we support. We give it a true "thumbs up."

OTHER SIGNIFICANT
PROGRAMS/SERVICES

There are always programs and services that are considered unique and helpful. This section discusses the Young Plaza Ambassadors program, which provides exceptionally different programs to seven hundred middle schools around the country. This program was actually started for the guests of the Plaza Hotel in New York City, and it has become so successful that it now attracts membership from middle schools.

CampSource is a camp/program consulting firm that guides you to an appropriate program for your child.

YPA (YOUNG PLAZA AMBASSADORS PROGRAM)
Lyudmila Bloch, Director
Plaza Hotel
Fifth Avenue and 59th Street
New York, NY 10019
(212) 546-5495
www.plazaypa.com

QUICK TAKE: The Plaza Hotel is known for its rich history and its role as one of the leading hotels in New York City. The Young Plaza Ambassadors (YPA) program celebrates legendary Plaza adventures, as well as reinforces and develops children's leadership and cultural skills. In the spirit of the hotel's dedication to excellence, the Plaza developed a program to help educate a new generation of sophisticated and cultured young people.

AGE REQUIREMENT: 6–16

DATES: Year round

FEES: Free to all Plaza guests traveling with children and staying for at least two nights. Nonguest membership, $150.00/year.

BACKGROUND: The YPA began in 2000 and has received rave reviews from every publication in which it has been reviewed.

DESCRIPTION: The YPA is a self-guided exploration that connects traveling families with cultural landmarks, museums, retailers, restaurants, and other exciting New York attractions. Members are equipped with VIP passes, priority admissions, complimentary tickets, and *Home Alone* sundaes (served on request).

The program offers a variety of educational activities, such as gourmet cooking classes, etiquette instructions, and veterinary workshops ("Junior Vet Clinic"). On their first visit to The Plaza, the children receive "welcome kits" with a YPA wallet, Plaza dollars, discount coupons, gifts from various partners, as well as planning services (i.e., personal shopping help at FAO Schwartz, a calendar of events, and an entertainment schedule) that make it easy for families to explore New York and its kid-friendly venues. The YPA's etiquette classes may seem outdated, but how often have you been in a business meeting or situation and felt clueless about using the right fork?

OUR TAKE: It is a program like no other. It is fun and the classes emphasize skills that a child can use daily.

OUR RECOMMENDATION: More than 6,000 individual members enjoy the YPA program to date, including students from 7,000 middle schools in the New York tristate area. Call them when you are in New York City, and see what they have cooking . . . gourmet cooking, that is! This program is an experience that you won't forget.

CAMPSOURCE
Camp Consulting and Referral Service
Abby Shapiro, Director
92 Deborah Road
Newton, MA 02459
(888) 985-CAMP (2267)
info@campsourcenet.com

QUICK TAKE: CampSource is a remarkable service that takes the time to match children with the best program available to them, based on their personalities, interests, talents, and abilities. It is a great place to begin when looking for a special experience for your child. The amazing part of the service is that Abby Shapiro, the director, is there not just to make the sale, but she is present throughout the course of the program to fix any problems. So not to worry if a camp experience isn't working for your child during his or her stay. Shapiro will work with you to solve any and all concerns.

BACKGROUND: CampSource is a free service dedicated to helping you find the best possible match between a summer program and your child. The agency's main goal is to "help parents understand which summer experience is best suited for their children." CampSource makes it a top priority to learn everything about the child and how he or she wants to spend the summer before spending time with both the parents and child to further understand their needs.

DESCRIPTION: CampSource experts have been able to establish relationships with directors by talking with them all winter and visiting them all summer. The result is first-hand knowledge to pass along to parents.

OUR TAKE: We have interviewed several parents who have used the service and they raved. CampSource is a good way to navigate the hundreds of programs out there. Abby Shapiro, the director, takes her work seriously. She is one of the best in the business, and we got the feeling that she seriously cares about the child after her placement. We give it a rave review.

RECOMMENDATION: Many parents we have contacted have given high marks to this service. We also contacted other comparable services, which did not follow through on camp suggestions, counseling services, and so on. Many of the other services lack the experience of CampSource. Shapiro's staff has years of experience, which makes it easier for you to find the perfect program to fit your child's interests at no cost. CampSource is dedicated to finding the best summer programs for hundreds of kids across the country. That's what its promotional material states . . . and we definitely agree.

INDEX